LONDON
A PRIVATE VIEW

Geoffrey Fletcher

Stoney Street, Southwark

LONDON
A PRIVATE VIEW

Geoffrey Fletcher

CASSELL

Cassell Publishers Limited
Artillery House, Artillery Row
London SW1P 1RT

First published 1990

British Library Cataloguing in Publication Data
Fletcher, Geoffrey
London: a private view.
1. London. Description & travel, 1990
I. Title
914.21′0485
ISBN 0-304-31670-9

This book has been set in Baskerville and Perpetua.
Printed and bound in Great Britain by
The Bath Press, Avon

Contents

List of Illustrations

1

Barbers' Shops

NOT ALL barbers are clever and smart, as Figaro asserts of himself. Some indeed are so unsmart that their talkativeness has driven me from their saloons, a wanderer in search of less loquacious operators. Haircutting is a horror to me any time, but never more than when I am obliged to reply to questions about the Cup Final, the Test Match or Wimbledon, spectacles that I have never witnessed and in which I have no interest.

After many abortive trials, I found in the purlieus of Fleet Street a man who is the reverse of these demon barbers. We have a perfect *modus vivendi*: beyond 'Same as usual?', to which I answer 'Yes', nothing is said: it has the brevity of Lord Rosebery's monosyllabic order at Lock's – a mere opening of the door and shouting 'Hat!'

Yet barbers have their mysteries. Everybody knows that a striped pole is a relic of the days when barbers also practised blood-letting, once a popular cure-all, but why in the north of England do they repair umbrellas? Nor was Poll Sweedlepipe alone in combining bird fancying with shaving, though cage birds are admittedly becoming rarer these days in barber shops. A canary hung up in the window to enjoy the sun was a primary attraction to me at 'The Saloon' in King's Cross Road. The Saloon is still in business, still with its charming gold and blue Edwardian lettering on the fascia, but the little yellow bird is gone and his place taken by a huge lemon-scented geranium. Such establishments are to be cherished in these degenerate days of trendy, epicene hairdressing emporiums. The greatest loss in London was the demise of 'The Baltic Saloon', Leadenhall Street. Nothing had been changed since the days of King Edward: the walls were papered with Lincrusta of an *art nouveau* pattern, above which was a frieze of formalised roses, and there was a plethora of mirrors and mahogany, marble and brass, bentwood chairs and cakes of shaving soap, for they used shaving mugs at the 'Baltic', as was proper. The only barber's I have ever seen excelling it was one in Genoa near the Porta Soprana: this had curved washbasins, curlicue painted cupboards, fantastic electric light fittings like bluebells – all of the 1890s and as *fin de siècle* as a poem by d'Annunzio. But on my last visit, it had gone the way of all flesh.

In Italy, the barber's shop is properly understood and taken seriously. It is, in fact, a club, without subscription and without blackballing. Like the pharmacies, you find one every few yards, thus providing for two of the great needs of Italians – self-medication and talk. 'Forward-One's' is the only concern I know in London where this club-like atmosphere exists. Even so, it is merely because the clients are mostly old-age pensioners and garrulously inclined; the talk consists entirely of complaints and mothy reminiscences of the General Strike or black-out experiences or of the country going to the dogs. 'Forward One's' is a husband-and-wife outfit. I fancy he was once a Naval barber and she a Wren; they have that period flavour hanging over them. The wife spends her days in a little upright booth like a sentry box, dispensing combs, razor blades and French letters which her partner calls 'requisites'. The moment I wait for is when a client wants a shampoo. The husband, flicking superfluous hair away, straightens himself up, clicks his fingers and gives the command 'Forward One!', at which summons the wife steps smartly from the box, pours water from a Victorian ewer on the customer's head and performs the ablutions. You get that you cannot do without this period pantomine; it is like the running of one's tongue over a defective tooth simply to jar the nerve. What's more, 'Forward One's' has a familiar outside, and these I cherish. Such figures are examples of the purest popular art. Wherever you find them, each appears to be done by the same primitive artist. The figures all wear a white coat and hold up a board with the legend 'Shave Sir?' or some such utterance. They all have dreadful eyes, hair parted in the centre and a Clark Gable moustache. Like Forward One and his spouse, they are tomorrow's antiques – perhaps even today's.

2

The Queen of Ely Place

WHEN THE medieval tiles, Flemish and of the thirteenth century, were discovered at St Etheldreda's, I went down to the Queen of Ely Place to see for myself; not that I needed an incentive, for the whole area of Ely Court and Ely Place, occupying the site of the town house and garden of the Bishops of Ely, with St Etheldreda as its relic, is an old favourite lounging place of mine, anyway. There is the added charm of 'The Mitre', cheek by jowl with the church, a satisfactory arrangement ministering in one plot to both spiritual and bodily requirements. I expected but a handful of tiles, and was astonished to find a long south-to-north paved area of glazed red, black, green and yellow tiles, abutting on the footings of the original cloister wall, found under a yard of soft earth when the floor of the canteen was taken up for reconstruction. What is fascinating is that the tiled passage (part of one side of the medieval cloister) may well be continued under the pavement of the back courtyard of the Mitre and then make a left-hand turn into Mitre Court – following the walls of the sixteenth-century pub and returning deep below the court in the foreground of my drawing. If so, then those who cut through Ely Court either to Ely Place or – preferably – to the Mitre are walking over more of London's buried treasure.

St Etheldreda, a king's daughter, died about 679, the abbess of the convent of Ely: her church, once the chapel of the bishop's palace, dates from the late thirteenth century, and is one of the few of medieval date ceded to the Roman Catholic persuasion. The chapel with its crypt below forms a relic of antique value. Its preservation is astonishing: as Ely Palace, once among the most magnificent of episcopal residences in London, decayed, so the chapel was used for a variety of purposes, undreamt of by its builders: a tavern in the seventeenth century, a school in the early part of the nineteenth, and then in December, 1843, it was opened for the Welsh community of the Established Church. Much of the original window tracery had by that time disappeared, though a great deal of the original stonework and carving remains in the interior. In 1874, the chapel was bought for the Roman Catholics.

The Mitre, Ely Court

Shakespeare must have known the now vanished Bishop's Palace well. In Richard II, he represents the death there of John of Gaunt, 'time honoured Lancaster' in 1399, and its gardens are recalled by the famous words of Gloucester to the Bishop in June, 1483. Shakespeare makes him say:

'My lord of Ely, when I was last in Holborn,
I saw good strawberries in your garden there;
I do beseech you, send for some of them!'

Ely Palace finally disappeared in the eighteenth century, when the levelled grounds were built over to form the present Georgian (and neo-Georgian in places) street in the early 1770s. It still had its curfew, and the porters' lodges replaced the old gatehouse. From the gateway or the palace itself remains a fragment – the bishop's mitre, carved in stone, built into the wall of the Mitre Tavern.

3
Seven Dials

HAVE BEEN looking at some old sketches of mine made in Seven Dials in 1945, and am astonished at the changes that have taken place, even in that much-altered district. Who now remembers the tea and lemonade stall under a big umbrella in Upper St Martin's Lane, outside the Regency stables where the Thorn Electric building now stands? It was an outfit straight out of Mayhew's London. And in West Street close by, strategically placed with admirable foresight by the Victorians, was a splendid cast-iron urinal, topped by a rich lamp. The street sweepers, latter-day representatives of the little private brigade Mr Ruskin employed in St Giles's High Street, were also picturesque and sported low-crowned, broad-brimmed hats. Then there was the print shop, now a barber's, in Tin Pan Alley, where one could buy engravings after Turner and other topographical prints for next to nothing, to the distant sound of a tinkling piano in a music publisher's office! Best of all was the Swiss–German café in St Giles's High Street, a relic of the Kaiser's Berlin and King Edward's London in combination. Four old Germans in white moustaches and aprons were stationed behind the long marble-topped counter, and each would pass your order for smoked sausage and sauerkraut to the other, like buckets of water at a fire, to the last man who executed it. Today I cannot even work out where it stood: goodbye to Berlin!

Yet the Victorians, themselves, initiated the changes that have swept away much of the interest from St Giles's Parish and the Dials. First came the cutting of New Oxford Street by Pennethorne – a move designed to get rid of some of the slums of the notorious Rookery; later came Shaftesbury Avenue and Charing Cross Road, followed by extensive developments in the late 1950s.

Even so, there are many interesting fragments left – enough to justify a tour after reading the two essays by Dickens, 'Seven Dials' and the piece, 'Monmouth Street', in *Sketches by Boz*. Some of the old Dials architecture of the eighteenth and early nineteenth centuries remains in Monmouth Street. On one façade can still be read in faded letters the legend

B. FLEGG
EST. 1847

Saddler and Harness Maker. Large Stock
of second hand Saddlery & Harness
Horse Clothing

And in the northern half of Monmouth Street – beyond the central area where the Seven Dials monument once stood – where its successor, a replica, will stand eventually – you find more writing on the wall, that of a long-vanished hatter's next to the Shaftesbury Hotel in what was once Great St Andrew's Street. Shelton Street, for part of its length, also retains some old architecture of the parish – the old shop fronts of humble aspect, in front of which the soft ice cream and hamburger men load up. Finest of all in Shelton Street (worth going a long way to see if you care about old London shop fronts) are some late Georgian premises with charming Gothic traceries in shallow arched windows to the ground floor 'shop', the whole painted Brunswick green, as it should be, and a bit of Regency ironwork on the steps.

In all this change, however, St Giles in the Fields Church remains the same, wonderfully preserved, beautifully and lovingly maintained. I often think that, though Flitcroft took Gibbs's St Martin's ostensibly as his model, he improved in some respects on his prototype, especially the ceiling, which, being less ornate, seems more successful. The most interesting approach – for then the church comes suddenly into view – is along Flitcroft Street, twisty and narrow, and ending at the dramatic, Roman-style gate, with its curious lunette of the Last Judgement.

> *'Hearts as pure and fair*
> *May beat in Belgrave Square*
> *As in the lowly air*
> *Of Seven Dials'*

says W. S. Gilbert. But the air is no longer lowly, having been purged of all but the fumes of petrol, and the indigent inhabitants of the parish, forever skirmishing with Peelers, poverty or the workhouse, have gone to where neither lemonade stalls nor cast-iron island lavatories can afford them solace. In their place are coming the owners of expensive coffee bars and boutiques, tip-top trend setters with months of jet life in front of them; the old bum-sick quarter is going for a Burton.

4

In the Steps of T. T. Riceyman

ARNOLD BENNETT once advised a friend of mine that the way to write a successful novel was to begin with a spectacular opening; the reader, electrified, would then read on – read on to almost anything, even a telephone directory, Bennett maintained. I cannot recall, however, any work of Bennett in which he put this precept into practice. My favourite novel, *Riceyman Steps*, which I have been reading once again, not only begins with a slow movement, but also continues that way throughout its length. It is, in fact, to an extraordinary degree a written instead of a painted Sickert – a Camden Town or Islington Sickert, in which two figures, carefully contrived to seem accidentally arranged, act out a joyless, dreary relationship in a stale interior, redeemed only by the sunlight which filters through the cheap lace curtains. Human beings are to me essentially boring and uninteresting; hence my belief that they only fulfil the non-entity of their lives and achieve their natural negation in these spectral circumstances.

Henry Earlforward, proprietor of his late uncle's bookshop, T. T. Riceyman's, is pure Sickert; so is the woman he married – Violet, owner of the confectioner's opposite; so are all the inhabitants of Riceyman Square. Life for them, in 1919, was what it had always been – an epic of survival with collapse ever teetering round the edges. Something of this still remained when I first knew Riceyman Square (Granville Square) in the 1940s. Old men still staggered to Rowton House for a nightly kip. The houses were almost as shabby and slatternly as Bennett described them. Tram cars ground along the King's Cross Road until 5 March 1938, the trolley buses which replaced the trams themselves running for the last time on 31 January 1961. The semi-circle of houses, Gwynn Place, at the foot of the steps, with its chord formed by King's Cross Road, were relics of war-time bombing, awaiting final demolition. Riceyman's second-hand bookshop, with a window on King's Cross Road and one in Gwynn place, on the right hand as you faced the steps, was little more than rubble; so, too, the confectioner's on the opposite corner. Ancient women of Clerkenwell trundled heavy bags along the grimy thoroughfare in front of the terrace – peeling like a

18

Riceyman Steps

plane tree's bark at that period – that stands on the site of Bagnigge Wells, and from a hoarding the Ovaltine girl, bonny and buxom, a Polly Peachum, triumphantly held up a tin of her beverage from a background of corn and meadowland. 'Here,' she was saying, 'is health.'

Having re-read the novel, I decided to revisit Riceyman on a day of soft September sunshine, with a suitable hint of melancholy in the air. Horses were being unloaded at the King's Cross Police Station – a valuable period touch; the building has been cleaned and fitted out with a rose garden, but otherwise remains grimly Victorian, as Riceyman's customers knew it. The terraces are now cleaned up and refurbished for the most part. Those on the north side, turned into flats, have lost their vines planted in the 1840s. Frederick Street, running up to Gray's Inn Road, has been so rehabilitated that it seems now to belong to Leamington or Cheltenham. I was pleased to see a horse and cart; it was as though things were being staged for me to show that all was not lost. Of course, the gasping, seedy men had quite gone; some few years ago, 'Rowton House' turned itself into 'The Mount Pleasant Hotel', for indigence, yellow soap and carbolic had become entirely old hat. Gwynn Place is nowadays screened by a modern block, 'The London Ryan Hotel'; taxis and big cars are parked in Riceyman's backyard. The steps of granite with a mid-way plateau of Yorkshire flagstones are unaltered; a cat sat there, scrutinising me closely as it washed its ears. The pedimented, late Regency style houses had form, Bennett conceded, though they were extensively cracked and dilapidated. Today, they are distinctly smart, forgetting, like 'Rowton House', a mouldy past. Modern mothers with squeaky kids sat in the sun in the centre garden, but even so the past would not be gainsaid: an elderly dame in decayed slippers and a 1920s print apron asked me what I was looking for. Of course, the milk cans had long since gone from the area railings – the Welsh dairy in nearby Lloyd Square went in for bottled milk at a very early date – and you must not expect to see a pasteboard Gothic church – the yellow brick St Andrew's – for that, like the so-called house of the Virgin at Loreto, had been miraculously transported from elsewhere.

You don't know Riceyman Steps, King's Cross Road? Best hunting-ground for books in London!

5
Mr Ruskin's Tea Shop

Most of London's literary landmarks have been written about *ad lacrimabundus*, so to speak: little remains to be told. But there is one of much interest and very little known, except to advanced students, and that is Mr Ruskin's tea shop at 29, Paddington Street, Marylebone. The street is cut into halves, forming four blocks, by the gardens formerly St George's burial ground. (Here, incidentally, you can admire a curiosity – a classic mausoleum with hanging baskets of geraniums depending from its cornice – a fantasy that would have appealed to Rex Whistler.) Probably because the street was so cut up, it has not been considered worth while to renumber it, and so the numbers run consecutively. As these have not changed since 1856, there is no difficulty in identifying No 29 on the corner of Chiltern Street. The shop, modernised, is now a greengrocery, but the whole of the building above, including the balconies, and the side door, is as Ruskin knew it.

His social writings were the result of his vast indignation on behalf of oppressed creatures, human or animal, but they were considered unintelligible by most of his contemporaries – considered fantastic, unworkable, Socialist – though they were none of these. An artist and art critic has no business, so his opponents said, to meddle with social reform: cobbler, stick to your last! Ruskin's contributions to the charity of England were not, however, to be confined to writing, which is easily done and costs nothing. Hence his purchase of property in Paradise Place and Freshwater Place, in the then slums of Marylebone, reconditioning and letting them to the very poor at the lowest possible rents. This successful experiment led to another, 'The Tea Shop', which was not so, in spite of the sign painted by Arthur Severn, the old china in the window and two of his old servants as shop assistants. Ruskin's own dry comment on the fortunes of the enterprise could not be bettered. He says:

> I set up a tea shop at 29 Paddington Street to supply the poor in that neighbourhood with pure tea, in packets as small as they chose to buy, without making a profit on the subdivision – larger orders being of course equally

acceptable from anybody who cares to promote honest dealing. The result of this experiment has been my ascertaining that the poor only like to buy their tea where it is brilliantly lighted and eloquently ticketed...I resolutely refuse to compete with my neighbouring tradesmen either in gas or rhetoric...but I believe none of these circumstances have checked my trade so much as my own procrastination in painting my sign. Owing to that total want of imagination and invention...I could not for months determine whether the said sign should be of a Chinese character, black upon gold; or a Japanese, blue upon white; or of pleasant English, rose colour on green; and still less how far legible scale of letters could be compatible, on a board only a foot broad, with lengthy enough elucidation of the peculiar offices of 'Mr Ruskin's tea-shop'. Meanwhile, the business languishes....

These were the days when low-priced tea was usually made up from leavings, bought from hotels at second hand, dried with the addition of a pinch of fresh tea and of carbonate of soda – a brew of tannin fit to turn the lining of the stomach into hide.

Later, of course, came the era of the big tea companies – The Queen's, Horniman's, Lipton's and the rest – whose large-scale operations enabled them to market good teas at an economical price. But I doubt whether the tea or its price had much to do with the short life of Mr Ruskin's business. I fancy it was the rarified, artistic, aesthetic character of the tea shop that frightened the poor customers away.

6
Where Greek meets Greek

T SEEMS to me that tourmasters offer synthetic fare – building Rome in a day, Florence before lunch, London in an hour – not from failure to understand what travelling is, but because they know that their clients only want to make unfavourable comparisons with home, and to get back there as quickly as possible. Yet my tour of Greece – Greece in London – is almost as good as the real thing – in fact, it is the real thing, and very cheap, with the optional extras thrown in for nothing.

In antiquity, the Greeks were great colonists; more recently, their colonisation of London was mainly in three waves; first after the upheavals of the 1920s, next following the unemployment of the 1950s and again after the troubles in Cyprus. First they settled in Soho and Charlotte Street, then Camden Town and so into Finsbury Park and the never-never lands beyond. Mediterranean peoples do not as a rule entertain great expectations, so that in starting a new life in the northern sea, they cannot have been much dismayed to find the streets of London paved not with gold, but instead with coppers. Still, they have shaken down, found little contrivances to make a living and got their children to speak English more easily than themselves, and though remaining a somewhat enclosed community, they have added interest and texture to London life.

Obviously my tour starts at the British Museum with the Parthenon frieze (the only school of art that G. F. Watts attended), so overwhelming in thought, design and execution, so far beyond comparison with anything else on earth, that the authorities, with superb gesture, let you see it gratis – rightly, for one must either pay a small fortune or pay nothing, anything in between would be intolerable. From here, one walks to St Pancras Church, where the hexastyle prostyle portico is finely copied from the Erectheum. The shadows cast between the intercolumniations are those of nineteenth-century scholarship, but still put us into the Greek mood, though the caryatid porches leading to the vaults have clumpy Amazons only distantly resembling the charming Korai of the Acropolis. (Here, before catching the bus to Camden is space for regret that the Doric propylæum went from Euston Square.)

Church, politics and family are the cornerstones of Greek life: they are as evident around Plender and Pratt Streets as at home. Camden has three Orthodox churchs: St Andrew's, Kentish Town (odd to see ancient, walnut-faced women, shrouded in black, emerging from a Gothic Revival church), SS. Comas and Damianos and All Saints down the perspective of Pratt Street. Nothing could be more suitable for the Orthodox rite than the Greek revival, All Saints, notable for its Easter procession and designed, like St Pancras, though in a severer style, by the Inwoods in 1824. The interior shows little trace of its former use as an Anglican church, when it was dedicated to St Stephen. There are great glass chandeliers, a glittering of icons and a pervading atmosphere of Byzantine solemnity, hierarchical and timeless. The holy faces eye one uncomfortably, searchingly: you feel they know you to be hare-brained and lightweight. You can buy your own icons in Plender Street – the modern ones of silver or silver foil – and a variety of other Greek productions – pottery cooking utensils, money boxes, fruit, books, vegetables and wine – even olive branches.

'The Paphos' is the restaurant I know best. I used to take my dog there, and, though no coward, he would find it convenient to get under the table when the menfolk would get up an extempore dance or become excited over a game of cards. It was very simple, then – imported straight from a Greek village – with an unsophisticated menu, scrubbed tables and home dress-making going on at the back. Straight from the village also are the old people, ambling along against a background of peeling stucco – the women in black woollens, the men with cloth caps. In my travels in Greece, I saw more cloth caps than olive trees, giving me a queer disorientated idea of actually being in Rochdale or Huddersfield, and one of relief that such garments were – presumably – not in use in the time of Pericles. Cloud-capped, but not cloth-capped Olympus – for otherwise the Parthenon could never have been!

7
The Reds and the Green

N THE wall of No 18 Farringdon Lane is a square tablet with the simple words 'Clerks' Well'. If you look through the adjoining window, you will see the well itself, recently restored and exposed to view; the water still flows under its huge six-sided wooden cover. On the wall above, a nineteenth-century cast-iron inscription informs us that here 'the Parish Clerks of London in remote Ages annually performed sacred Plays. That Custom caused it to be denominated Clerks Well and from which this Parish derived its Name'.

Very little greenery remains on the Green beyond a few trees evincing a praise-worthy determination not to give in; other London greens – Turnham, Islington, Newington, Richmond – are the genuine article, or nearly so. But Clerkenwell Green has a unique atmosphere, retaining to a surprising extent a village-like character, in spite of the industrialisation which began with the clockmakers in the time of Christopher Pinchbeck. The Green was a favourite rendezvous for the many protest meetings of the 1880s, one of the contingents of the 'Bloody Sunday' fracas assembling there. But the atheists, the Socialist Leaguers, the agitators have vanished like an uneasy dream, without trace. Not all the commercial buildings are unprofitable. In Bowling Green Lane is one of the finest examples of Victorian commercial architecture in London, the offices of Messrs W. Notting, recently cleaned and proving how attractive nineteenth-century brickwork was when newly built. The façade, dated 1877, is divided into recessed panels by finely designed buttresses, with string courses of red brick marking the floor levels. Terracotta panels – the only decorative elements in the elevation – in triangular pediments complete a totally satisfactory composition – one that came easily to Victorians, but which would strain every nerve of a present-day architect to achieve. Hence, if you want a liberal education in the science of using simple materials to create a warehouse which is also a notable work of art, go to Bowling Green Lane.

The Green derives its architectural distinction from the Palladian-style 'Sessions House' of 1779 – it ceased to be a law court in 1919 – and the church of

Clerkenwell Close and church steps

St James, in the Wren manner, but with a distinctive quality of its own. There is also much good Georgian domestic work to be found on the perimeter, as in St James's Walk, and of the 1820s in Sekforde Street. On the Green is the pedimented Welsh Charity School of 1737, now the Marx Memorial Library; both Marx and Lenin used it when it was a revolutionaries' club, for, by that time, as I have just remarked, industrialised Clerkenwell Green had become a notable place for political demonstrations – the reds on the Green, so to say. The view from the seats where old men once bored each other to death with reminiscences of queues for razor blades and cigarettes is as fine as an old London print by Thomas Malton, and the Crown Tavern at the corner has a good display of nineteenth-century etched glass windows, proclaiming the special whiskies, rums and brandies to be obtained within.

In the seventeenth century, Clerkenwell Green and its surrounds was a desirable residential area for the well-to-do – a place of country houses such as 'Newcastle House' (built like St James's Church on the site of the suppressed nunnery, the cloisters of which followed the line of Clerkenwell Close) – country houses within a stone's throw of the City. Nor has the country been entirely snubbed out of countenance. There are green lawns round the church, and at Easter beds of daffodils and forsythia bravely showing under indigo skies. There are bees of portly size, already about their affairs, and the eccentric blackbird, ending his song with a cynical cackle. There are also young couples arm in arm, talking of the things they plan and taking the air, at lunch times. Than this could nothing be more appropriate, for it was here that Henry Carey, music master at Sadler's Wells, on such a wandering saw such a couple – the London 'prentice and his gal – was charmed with them, went home and wrote his evergreen, fragrant masterpiece, 'Sally in our Alley'.

8
Limehouse Views

SOME PEOPLE get their ideas from life, others from books; both are misleading. But I had the idea of a Limehouse wandering from a TV screening of a film, *Broken Blossoms* by D. W. Griffith, made in autumn, 1918. Lillian Gish starred as the forlorn waif who drudged for her adopted father, the boozer Battling Burrows, welterweight, of Pekin Street, Limehouse. The film, totally sentimental and melodramatic, was based on the first story in a pre-Great War book by Thomas Burke, *Limehouse Nights* – without doubt the worst book ever written on London and of unsurpassable corniness. The trouble was that Burke (who lived to write better books) was thoroughly gammoned by locals when he went slumming in search of sensational material. Certainly Chinatown was much rougher then than now. Still, the lurid bosh with which Burke was flannelled – opium dens, murders in blind alleys, Oriental revelry and devilish Chinese – was already stale. Limehouse, merely very poor and decaying, was about as sinister as a Methodist Sunday outing.

The wonder is that Griffiths could have got so much out of it, so much atmosphere, especially as his conception of Limehouse landscapes was so very approximate. All the old worn-out streets where Burke placed his characters were totally changed in the rebuildings of the 1930s and again after the last war. Limehouse Causeway, for instance, is nowadays nothing but flats – not a joss house in sight. But there are Chinamen – more than on my last visit; in fact, when the great exodus of the Chinese began over a dozen years ago – to create a new updated Chinese quarter westward in Lisle and Gerrard Streets – I began to fear that an Oriental in Limehouse would be as difficult to find as a Fascist in Italy. But they are still here in Chinatown and with them more restaurants than ever, taking the place of my former favourite, 'The Old Friends', which stood on the corner of Mandarin Street: the site is now grassed over and turned into a feeble open space.

Here and there bits of the old Limehouse remain among the architectural face-lifts. Francis and Chris Walters still conduct their funerals from the old place

28

opposite Limehouse Church. There is a strip of early nineteenth-century terrace surviving in the West India Dock Road, though all opposite in Pennyfields is bang up to date. Pekin Street, where Battling Burrows was domiciled, is nothing but post-1945 flats. Neither Burrows nor his punch bag drudge or the Chinese boy who befriended her would recognise any of it, and a sight of the girls in tights, with wiggly bottoms and green hair, the prams and the flash cars, would prove to them that they were somehow in the wrong league.

I strolled down to the river, to the 'Grapes' pub – the 'Six Jolly Fellowship Porters' of *Our Mutual Friend*. I was glad to see how well looked after are these old houses in Narrow Street nowadays. They were saved only at the last minute, and rightly for they are the best, St Anne's Church excepted, of all that is left of old Limehouse. A sign of changed times is the exclusive wine bar in Narrow Street, and sleek cars where once the horses munched their midday oats; the old W. W. Jacobs waterfront life has vanished like a river mist. Limehouse nights are nights at the discotheque or the cash and carry and the newer opiate is the telly.

Clink prison bollard, Bankside

9

Italians in Holborn

N ITALIAN woman got into conversation with me in the cathedral at Bologna, and finding that I came from London, declared her hatred of the English for what they had done to Italy during the war. With some heat, I said, '*Momento! Ma via!* You have it by the wrong handle! Musso and his thugs were your enemies – and ours. We English have an ancient and famous attachment to Italy. We have certificates to prove it. Mazzini lived among us; thousands of Italians still do so – in London's Little Italy and elsewhere.'

I thought of this conversation in the porch of St Peter's Italian Church recently, when looking up the details of its famous procession – the *Processione della Madonna del Carmine* – held in July and often enough in a torrid temperature that Italy could hardly rival. In the porch is a monument to the Great War dead of the parish – a long list of names eloquent of the size of the Italian community of that time. Undoubtedly, they were almost all poor men – mosaic workers, organ grinders, waiters, ice-cream men who doubled up with chestnuts in the winter – yet the names, given resonance by the genius of the language, are impressive and noble. Luigi Piazza – Lorenzo Colosso – Aquilino Ferrari – they might be tremendous figures from the Renaissance or from the cast of a Neapolitan opera. In fact the colony, originally bounded by Clerkenwell Road, Farringdon Road and what is now Rosebery Avenue, was recruited largely from Southern Italy – the Mezzogiorno. Its greatest concentration was about 1900, in the maze of slum property around Warner Street, Eyre St Hill, Back Hill, Saffron Hill and so on. The *Daily Telegraph* in November 1903 reported the coming change – the demolition of insanitary overcrowded courts and ill-lit alleys to make way for warehouses and industrial buildings. Therefore, though there is still something of Little Italy left, the community is now widespread and the Italians come from all over London to do honour to the Virgin.

Some of the vanished tenements were run by a *Padrone*, who would import a houseful of poor Italians to work for him, he supplying accommodation (of a kind) and taking a hefty slice of their meagre earnings, and his dependants

Mazzini's House, Laystall Street, Clerkenwell

would include beggar boys. Mary Barton in Mrs Gaskell's novel shares her supper with a destitute little Italian boy and his white mouse in the Manchester of the 1840s.

Changes are still taking place; the Roman Catholic school of St Catherine Labouré at the corner of Herbal Hill, where so many immigrant children learned English, has only recently been converted to other uses; it is now a ballet school. Yet those poor Italians knew how to run a procession – as they still do – and on the great day came out with holy pictures on crumbling walls, flights of pigeons, a triumphal arch. St Peter's (though designed by an English Protestant architect) is instant Italy: Ionic columns, confessionals, mosaics, old women in black and that feature without which no Italian church is complete, the aspidistra. Some of the Italians, after making enough capital, went home, drawn irresistibly by *campanilismo*, the burning desire for one's own church tower; others, such as the Gatti brothers, stayed on to become famous restaurateurs; few of them intermarried with their English neighbours.

But not only is the quarter Italian, it is also Dickensian, and figures largely in *Oliver Twist*. Vine Hill, formerly Vine Street, was once named Mutton Hill, and it was along it that Oliver was taken on his way to the Police Court in Hatton Garden. At the bottom of the hill is the Field Lane Ragged School and Night Refuge in which Dickens took a great interest. Though no longer either a ragged school or refuge, it remains intact, its name carved in stone on the walls and picked out in faded letters on the battlemented tower, a very pure example of Victorian institutional architecture. Celebrated men have long indulged a habit of alleging a lowlier original than the facts warrant, but who, I wonder, would go so far as to lay claim to education at a ragged school?

In Laystall Street there is a plaque on the wall of a barber's shop, where Mazzini once had rooms. This is not the only memorial to Mazzini in London: another is in Gower Street North, and a third, in bronze, is on the wall of a jeweller's shop at the southern end of Hatton Garden. For Mazzini, surely ranking in greatness with Dante and Michelangelo, resided for many years in London, a city that he came gradually but certainly to love. Perhaps his idealism, his belief in the possibilities of humanity, visible on every page of *The Whole Duties of Man*, expected too much of our shortcomings. But he was practical also, and in his rooms in Hatton Garden he conducted his own school for ignorant, starveling Italian boys who were even poorer than himself. Mazzini, a political exile seeking refuge, arrived here in 1837. Small groups of Italians had been around London for centuries – craftsmen skilled in plaster work, mural decorators, Canaletto in Soho, but the arrival of migratory Italians was a feature of the 1820s onwards, most of them at first from the northern provinces. A distinctive class, poor and largely illiterate, found their way in increasing numbers up to the end of the century, and these originated from Southern Italy. Many of these were boys, as I have said, turned on to the streets, usually to beg, and obliged to hand over their miserable earnings to the *padrone* in return for lodgings. As the years passed, fresh immigrations and intermarriage resulted in a more settled character for the area, and with London-born Italians what had at first been a colony largely of young male Italian expatriots solidified into a permanent community.

Why the Italian hospital was built in 1884 in Queen Square, so far from its patients, I have never understood. Nor have I ever been clear about why the Italians established themselves in and around Back Hill, Saffron Hill (cruelly misnamed, even then) and Eyre Street Hill, though the central position of the area and its run-down condition is the probable explanation. Another mystery is – what exactly were the plaster figures manufactured there and hawked by the children on the London streets? They could not have been of simpering saints and madonnas of the kind found throughout Italy, since these would hardly arouse much enthusiasm in our Protestant capital, nor would selling such figures amongst themselves be greatly profitable. Were they – I ask myself without much hope of an answer – the ancestors of those dreadful Alsatians and cherry boys that I used to see through the lace curtains of Bermondsey parlour windows? Like the Italian piano-organ and hurdy-gurdy men and the vendors of water-ice or hokey-pokey, they have vanished from the earth. Of these cottage industries little remains but the mosaics in lavatories and in the entrances to London pubs.

There were, too, Italians male models domiciled in Little Italy, the exiled counterparts of those who, awaiting hiring by artists, whiled away their vacant hours on the Spanish Steps in Rome. I knew one of these nineteenth-century emigrant models when I was at the Slade in the late 1940s. He had arrived in Little Italy as a penniless young man, and found work as an Academy model. He was about ninety when I knew him and still active. He remembered clearly posing for Millais as 'The Forerunner' in that rum late painting of a John the Baptist sort of figure, wearing nothing but a wooden cross and a loin cloth.

In June 1988, I took a party of Italian schoolchildren from Manfredonia round London. We toured Little Italy on a Saturday afternoon. In St Peter's was an Italian wedding, though with confetti thrown instead of the sugared almonds in Italy. There was a plump, overdressed, confident bride, a self-conscious bridegroom, uneasy in his new shiny suit, and tearful old women in black. My young friends recognised it all, instantly – a proof of its genuineness – and what intrigued them most was this strange double character of a grimy London street on the outside of the church, but inside, *Italia! Italia!*

10
For Want of a Shoe

IF ST PANCRAS, merged into the greater borough of Camden in 1965, was never, like Oxford, the home of lost causes – in fact, the reverse – it was, and still is, the home of unlikely survivals. One of these is the King's Road Forge in Pancras Way, with the words painted in faded letters on the lintel. Even its name is a survival, for the King's Road disappeared in 1937, giving place to Pancras Way: there was quite a lot of renaming in the area about that period, when the neighbouring Great College Street changed to Royal College Street in 1939.

The forge's history seems largely undocumented, but it has been a blacksmith's shop at least since the turn of the century: the present owner tells me the deeds 'are on a huge piece of parchment, covered over with fine old lettering'. Looking through old sketchbooks, I notice that this is the third old London forge I have visited. There was Margrie's, who had to move from Cheyne Walk, Chelsea, because of redevelopment at the foot of Albert Bridge, and Mr Edwin Margrie remembered the strings of horses once brought in to be shod; and then there was Frost and Hayter's also in Camden Town, an old shop with traditional forge and anvil, but producing decorative iron work instead of the one-time farrier's craft of shoeing horses. It is the same story at the King's Road forge.

'It's mainly now railings, gates,' said the blacksmith, who was making a set of Victorian-style spearheaded railings and gates, 'staircases and things like that and basket grates. As recently as twenty years ago, the forge was going all day, every day. Now it's lit only once every so often. But there's a world of difference, however more expensive – and I'll show you – between the machine-made scroll work and the real blacksmith's work. The blacksmith's scroll work has slight variations, individuality, character. You can't press a button and then collect the ironwork that a machine turns out and say, "I made that."'

The blacksmith ferreted out a number of scroll formers from the collection of tools that covered the oxide-stained walls and explained, 'You warm a small amount of metal, put it in the scroll form and gradually pull it round to the shape, and finally there are small differences, one piece of ironwork compared with another – they're not all the same, like peas in a pod.'

I watched fascinated as he brought a baronial-sized fire grate into existence under his hands. Finally, he disinterred a trade card, the property of a long-gone owner of the forge, and handed it to me:

J. Scott

109 Kings Road Camden Town
Every virgin job guaranteed
100% original strength and finished as new

Metropolitan peanuts, Spitalfields

11
Bedford Park

THE ENGLISH, whatever their old reputation for trade, manufacture and literature – three oddly associated activities – have never been notable for significant art movements of the kind that blossom in regular progression in France. Yet the last century produced three – the chief and most original, Pre-Raphaelitism, then the Aesthetic Movement, which was strangled, so to say, by the sinister lax tendrils of *Art Nouveau*, the last named being a purely Scottish–English phenomenon, though exported to Vienna, Brussels and Paris and then reimported. Of these, only Pre-Raphaelitism was a conscious movement by a group of artists having a declared programme. The Aesthetic Movement, on the contrary, published neither manifesto nor syllabus. Although it had an assortment of sources – some of them seemingly unlikely to combine and blend – its pedigree was far from obvious. Like the Great Gatsby, it just arrived, or so casual observers might have thought, and, like Topsy, it just grew. Its chief architectural professors were W. E. Nesfield, E. W. Godwin and R. Norman Shaw; its chief motif was the sunflower, which became an absolute badge of the style, a mania even.

Shaw was a virtuoso in the Aesthetic or Queen Anne style: in it, he produced some of his most delightful and most interesting work: the pity is that his immense talents led him later to such horrors as New Scotland Yard and the immodest vulgarism that constituted Edwardian Baroque. The ingredients of the Aesthetic style in architecture were the tile-hung cottages of the Surrey villages, a hint of the old domestic architecture of Holland, a motif or two from Essex pargeting, one or two items from the classic vocabulary and a little something from Japan (mainly, the chrysanthemum ornament, which first appears – the shape of things to come – in Sir Frederick Leighton's house in Kensington). Gilbert, who poked fun at the excesses of the aesthetes in 'Patience', came to have his house designed by Shaw. The careful reader of the libretto of 'Patience' will detect a confusion of ideas (whether deliberate or not is impossible to say) between the 'stained-glass attitudes' of Rossetti–Burne-Jones Pre-Raphael-itism and the aestheticism of Whistler, Albert Moore and the rest, of which Oscar

The Tabard, Bedford Park

Wilde made himself the chief but least informed publicity agent. Shaw also designed Kate Greenaway's house in Hampstead. Here was a total consistency, for Kate Greenway's books along with those of Walter and Thomas Crane were the very embodiment of the Aesthetic period.

So, too, was Bedford Park, a visit to which is one of the most satisfactory expeditions to be made in London. It remains almost *virgo intacta*, almost but not quite. What is needed is to have the whole estate, started by an entrepreneur called J. T. Carr in the early 1870s, put back exactly as it was, preserved as a unique Victorian experience. It ought to be surrounded by a wall. Certainly I would banish all later excrescences – TV aerials, cars and vans. A condition of residence there would be to read Ruskin and Walter Pater, to admire only Pre-Raphaelite Brotherhood paintings and those of Rossetti, Burne-Jones and Fred Walker, to utilise no modern equipment and to think no modern thoughts. For to do otherwise is to live in a state of total disharmony with the architecture, the spirit of the place – to be a Philistine, unredeemed, irregular. If you venture there, you will find among the roads and avenues a most satisfactory collection of detached and semi-detached houses, superficially village-like, but in fact stylish, with varied windows, porches, balconies and decorations, all aimed at the mildly artistic, the genteelly refined middle classes of the period (not, of course, the Mrs Ponsonby-Tomkins of du Maurier's drawings). It is difficult to decide at this date exactly the kind of people who actually lived in these houses, all built under the Shaw influence if not actually by him, but the most famous resident was the actor–manager William Terris, who was stabbed to death by an out-of-work actor outside the stage door of the Adelphi theatre in 1897.

Two outstanding Shaw designs dominate Bedford Park. The Tabard Inn with its de Morgan tiles (and period wall papers recently reintroduced), gabled, picturesque in the manner of an old country town inn and unblushingly pretty is, like a Greenaway or Crane drawing, the ultimate essence of the period. Next to it, and forming a continuous façade, are the Co-operative stores of the garden suburb. They are now offices, but were, when opened, the world's first serve-yourself store. Opposite the Tabard is what I always consider the finest of all Shaw's buildings – the church of St Michael and all Angels. Given the problem – a self-concious, mildly arty garden suburb and a church to serve it – what style could possibly be employed to correspond, to coalesce? An adaptation of Wren would be too academic; Gothic Revival too dated; a simple Regency box as favoured by Methodists too out of place for a middle-class (but artistically enlightened) congregation of Anglicans. Shaw solved it brilliantly. Its sheer cleverness impresses me each time I visit it. His answer was to go back to Jacobean Gothic – more or less – the Gothic that, infiltrated with Renaissance elements, crept in to give historic English Gothic its quittance. Shaw provided, therefore, a late Perpendicular nave arcade, with an open timber roof, and excellent woodwork of Jacobean type, the whole design inside and out having an airiness and stylishness that carries complete conviction.

Now that London is becoming a city for tourists instead of a place to live and work in, there might be a future for organised tours of aesthetic London, taking in Chelsea, Mayfair, Kensington and even the old Board Schools.

Electric lamp standard, Brushfield Street, Spitalfields

12

Cloth Fair

GENERALLY SPEAKING, demolitions and rebuildings are not my scene – far from it. However, new rebuildings in Cloth Fair, in a style calculated to harmonise with the best that remains, is welcome enough, I think: the tatty war-damaged property had been a depressing sight for too long. What is so incredible (or not so incredible, perhaps, when one thinks of the vanished Clare Market and its replacement by Kingsway, most barren of all thoroughfares) is that the old houses of Cloth Fair were allowed to disappear in the face of commercial pressures early in the century: all, that is, except the very last of the garrison, the old gabled house which was saved in the 1930s by Lord Mottistone and his partner, Paul Paget – a noble act. When looking back on London through the medium of old drawings and photographs, I invariably marvel at the feebleness of the English in resisting demolitions, and wonder also that we have anything left in London.

Cloth Fair, built up after the dissolution of the monasteries, is an extraordinary example of this, for within living memory – that is up to just before the Great War – most of it and much of Bartholomew Close and their tributary alleys were a unique enclave of gabled houses of Elizabethan and early Jacobean date, with two ancient taverns, equally picturesque, 'The Blakeney's Head' in Bartholomew Close and the 'Dick Whittington' at the north-east corner of Cloth Fair, and a blacksmith's shop, which abutted the priory walls on the north transept side. There were curious gabled houses on both sides of the street, those on the south side backing into the churchyard garden, the site of the nave of the great priory church. A remnant of this scenic quality can still be found in the red-brick Georgian house of the verger which is built against the church walls, half-way down Cloth Fair. Farther down, at the corner of Kinghorn Street, is 'The Hand and Shears' pub. Here was annually held the curiously named Court of Pie Poudre or Pie Powder for the regulation of weights and measures and other matters during Bartholomew Fair. It was originally a three-day event for the retailing of cloth. As time went on, its original character changed into a sort of blend of Nottingham Goose Fair and the Derby, and it spread out of Cloth

Fair into the wide spaces of Smithfield, until eventually it was suppressed as a nuisance in 1855.

Massive and grand as it still is, St Bartholomew the Great is yet only a fragment (largely the choir, with the first bay of the nave) of the great mutilated priory church. The solemnity of the time-worn, time-stained Norman piers, triforium and clerestory and the absolute silence and peace of the place make it, I believe, the most precious architectural relic in London. Its restoration at the end of the nineteenth century by Sir Aston Webb was an outstanding example of sheer professional skill combined with the utmost feeling and respect for old work; not a stone, worked or unworked, was displaced unless absolutely inevitable. The two chief Gothic features are Rahere's tomb of the fifteenth century with traces of the original colour remaining and the oriel window of Prior Bolton over the south side of the choir – jammed unceremoniously into a Norman arch – with the prior's rebus, a bolt struck through a ton, in a panel below. Prior Bolton was the last but one to hold office, 1506–1532. He lived, therefore, in dangerous times, and his architectural works were undertaken when the Reformation was, so to speak, knocking at his door.

With it came the great sell-out, the priory and its hefty emoluments being sold up, the package deal including the revenues from Bartholomew Fair. Sad and bad enough, certainly, but the worse that followed is merely hinted at by the memorial stone on the wall of St Bartholomew's Hospital, naming a few only of the many saintly sufferers for the Protestant faith, to be read about in that veritable Domesday Book – Foxe's *Book of Martyrs*. I don't suppose anyone ever reads this horrifying chronicle nowadays, though it was once required reading in Protestant homes on Sundays, along with the Bible and the *Pilgrim's Progress* – and as for being burnt for truth's sake, we now have it on Government testimony, that smoking can seriously damage one's health!

13
Gas Lamps

SHERLOCK HOLMES, at the beginning of the adventure of 'The Copper Beeches' is reported as laying aside his copy of the *Daily Telegraph* and remarking that to the man who loves art for art's sake, the greatest pleasure is often got from its least important examples. As usual, he was right: his colossal intellect discerning what lesser intelligences fail to see – the importance of unimportant art. The very gas lamps that provided the atmospheric background necessary to the cosiness of the crimes in his casebook (gas light, a distracted female and fog in the square) might have been cited by him as examples. Fortunately, a comprehensive collection of these specimens of cast iron still remains – the successors to the Georgian wrought-iron work of link extinguishers and brackets for colza oil lamps of Mayfair.

Sometimes the two epochs are combined, as in the nineteenth-century gas lamp suspended over the entrance to Middle Temple Lane on a Georgian bracket; the voussoirs of the lintel behind and the Agnus Dei carved on the keystone form a harmonious whole often passed by without a second glance. But the finest of all are those along the Strand, 'the iron lilies' of Richard le Gallienne's poem. His description is not so affected as might be presumed from a *fin-de-siècle* poet: the standards, now electrified, have the sinuous grace of Turk's Head lilies, planted along the Strand in slender pots. The earlier standards of 1899, found in the West Strand and in other parts of St Martin's parish, are made entirely delightful by the bas-relief cartouche of St Martin dividing his cloak with the beggar; nothing could be finer than these.

Similar standards – there are some outside the Law Courts – are the City of Westminster type of 1902, a design modified from the earlier St Martin's pattern, the saint having been replaced by the City of Westminster's device: the saints were marching out. Even so, at this time, the St Pancras Council were responsible for another saintly lamp post – the stem and parts above being nothing, the pedestal or plinth everything, and having a well-modelled relief of the boy saint, St Pancras, in a pedimented niche of the kind seen on classical sarcophagi. A few lamps of this sort can still be found. For the connoisseur, the finest collection of

St Martin dividing his cloak, St Martin-in-the-Fields

gas lamps, apart from those in Covent Garden, are in Lincoln's Inn, and all very properly working on gas. There is an exceptional collection of slender pillar lamps and some rich individual ones, such as the one over the door of No 11 Stone Buildings – a choice specimen of a six-sided lantern finished with a noble finial and projecting on a plain strip-like bracket contrasting with the richness of the green and gold lantern: harmonious in every way, for greenish gold is the very colour of the living flame of the gaslight itself, infinitely preferable to the harsh impersonal light of electric lamps and imparting a kind of confidence about what goes on indoors.

Gas lamp, Covent Garden

Covent Garden and its surrounding streets are still gas lit, thanks to the respect for propriety and the vigilance of those who live and work in the area. There are, for instance, the two quite superb bracket ones under the portico of St Paul's Church, and the three fine ones all different in New Row. Better still are the Gothic lamps, elongated octagons with steep tops like those jutting from the waters of Venetian canals, in St Paul's churchyard garden.

Finest of all are the four great candelabra lamps, as magnificent and as self-assured as the Victorians themselves, at the east end of St Clement Dane's, behind the National Portrait Gallery (a shamelessly Baroque one this, topped with crown and cushion, and like its fellow at St Clement Dane's, lighting the way to the 'conveniences') and, lastly and richest, the pair in Trafalgar Square (sometimes ascribed mythically to Alfred Stevens) of 1878. They are rich with acanthus and swags and charming caryatid putti and the initials VR above winged and fish-tailed lions. Such zoological novelties did not worry our great grandfathers, for the British lion really ruled the waves, in Queen Victoria's golden days!

14
Pre-Raphaelite Stream

UCH AS I love drawing and painting architecture, there are times when I wish that I had followed up my schoolboy love – lasting unimpaired to this day – of the Pre-Raphaelites. Had I done so, I could have painted pictures like 'Autumn Leaves' (perhaps) or the Rossetti watercolours in which bright, mysterious figures walk where the briar rose springs up in the wild wood. Better still, I would have liked to consort with those concupiscent, long-necked women with copper-coloured hair who infested the house in Cheyne Walk, and painted them yearning for untasted amorous disillusions. Whenever I walk in spring sunshine among hedgerows, the aspect of things appears wonderfully like Pre-Raphaelite Brotherhood (PRB) paintings. There are the same viridian shadows in emerald grass, diversified by the bronze of last autumn's leaves, the shadows of primroses on their own foliage and a million lights from ivy leaves reflecting the sun's disk, all in sharp focus. It makes the retrospective landscape conventional, operatic, and post-Pre-Raphaelite painting merely clumsy daubs of paint. It is the same penetrative, almost physical joy in Nature which distinguishes Wordsworth as a poet and Ruskin as a critic, fused with that vague melancholy peculiar to the PRBs, a sense of unease which yet stops short of the defeating dejection of Coleridge.

These reflections occurred to me when I spent two days wandering along the Pre-Raphaelite stream, the Hogsmill, and drawing the eighteenth-century Upper Mill, a working flour mill as recently as 1952. The Hogsmill rises at Ewell Spring, pulsating under the road into its stone basin, where minnows dart in the shadows, and meanders a six-mile course to the Thames, willow-fringed and rural yet in places, in spite of the building development in the area in the 1930s.

Holman Hunt in his Pre-Raphaelite memoirs, which contain many charming references to 'our favourite haunt, Ewell', including a description of the Upper Mill and the flour-whitened men, says that the background for 'The Hireling Shepherd' was found a mile from the stream's source. Millais had to go farther afield to the meadows at Cuddington to find the material for his unforgettable

Upper Mill, Ewell

'Ophelia'. This was in the summer and autumn of 1851, a marvellous period of youth, work, gaiety and fulfilment, when the artists, visited occasionally by Pre-Raphaelite friends, were in digs at Worcester Park Farm, an area to be subsequently built up onwards from the 1890s, vividly recalled in Hunt's book and laconically jotted down at the time by Millais in a fragmentary diary.

Hunt had already as a student given effect to his attachment to Ewell in two paintings, a small one of the Hogsmill, now erroneously titled 'The Haunted Manor' (it is actually of the demolished old mill house) in the Tate, and a painting of St Mary the Virgin, a larger oil done before the old church, apart from the tower, was demolished. I had the unusual gratification of discovering this early Holman Hunt after the canvas had been living for years in reduced circumstances and, after cleaning, ensuring its future. The view of the Upper Mill from the mill stream is still entirely Pre-Raphaelite, with Tennysonian undertones. Chaffinches sing on the chestnut branches and the blackbird clutters his resentment at invasion of his privacy. The sunlight filters through on to vivid green undergrowth. Ivy climbs round windows and across the big door where the water wheel turned, barring it with its tendrils. In such a manner the ivy and brambles choke the closed door at which Christ knocks in Hunt's 'Light of the World' (also painted at Worcester Park Farm): the ancient sin in the heart of man that resists the summons of the Saviour.

15
London by the Yard

BY 'LONDON yards' I do not mean the domestic backyards, for example, those of Bermondsey, into which we gaze from the train at surprising collections of pigeon lofts, sunflowers, heroic trees and tin baths. Many of these homely yards, anyway, have become patios: to confess to having a backyard is an outward sign of an inward lack of grace. I mean those variously shaped and often interestingly named paved areas found all over London, often to be got at only through narrow entries, like Mason's Yard in St James's. Scotland Yard is, I suppose, the most famous London yard, as Fleet Street is the most famous street. What can be seen today amounts to little more than the dull late architecture of Norman Shaw. It was once, however, the London residence of the Scottish kings and of John Milton during his period as Latin Secretary to the Commonwealth. It interested the young Dickens enough to devote one of the *Sketches by Boz* to it, by which time Scotland Yard had become a coal wharf (seen in old drawings as an assembly of hefty timbers and picturesque sheds) with a small resident population and an eating house and wainscoted pub – the choicest spot, Dickens says, in the whole of the yard.

More atmospheric is Playhouse Yard, Blackfriars. In spite of his working life spent here, most parts of London associated with Shakespeare are peculiarly lacking in solid documentation, but here, as at Bankside, are certainties. Playhouse Yard is on the site of the Blackfriars Monastery – of the Dominicans or Black Friars. When the monastery was dissolved, part of the buildings were acquired by the actor, Burbage, who turned them into a theatre, where Shakespeare's company played during the winter – the 'Blackfriars', unlike the 'Globe' and the 'Rose', being roofed in – and Shakespeare himself had shares in the concern.

Bell Yard, whether you look up from Fleet Street to the Georgian group and the Union Bank (as it was when John Ruskin banked there) in Carey Street at the top or down in the direction of Temple Bar, has recommended vistas. South, I think, to Fleet Street is the best, for it shows most clearly the remarkable curiosity of the yard – a truce, as it were, in the Victorian battle of styles. The left-hand side

49

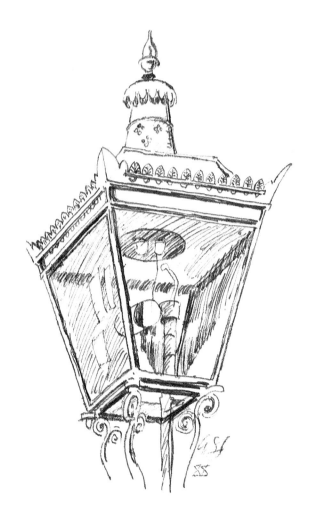

Gas lamp, Guildhall Yard

is entirely classical from the rear of the Law Society down to the Italianate building, once the Bank of England Law Courts Branch and now the offices of a Building Society; the right-hand side is the Gothic rear of Street's Law Courts, behind the grille of Verona-like wrought iron, and the view is closed by the bell tower of the Law Courts rising up in stages of white stone and red brick. Only the meanly designed modern lamps of the Westminster Council mar a complete harmony of contending styles, and they are easily overlooked, as they ought to

50

be. Star Yard, a northern continuation – we are now getting into the world of Jarndyce v. Jarndyce – is also a pleasing mixture of the sort that London keeps on hand for the pleasure of wanderers. Here, very well preserved, is one of the few remaining cast-iron urinals, painted a pleasing Dutch green and having a royal coat of arms in relief on the decorative panels – surely a flagrant case of *lèse-majesté!* If you are interested in old London crafts, you can glance in at the door of Ede and Ravenscroft's and watch the girls curling the wigs on wooden blocks.

Saffron Hill is the place to find Bleeding Heart Yard, so called from the sign of the bleeding heart of Mary Virgin, pierced by arrows, which once hung there. *The Ingoldsby Legends* describe how Lady Hatton was carried off by the Devil, her heart subsequently being found in the neighbourhood: the author, R. H. Barham, counsels us:

> '*The last bit of advice which I'd have you regard*
> *Is, don't go of a night into Bleeding Heart Yard.*'

Its chief claim to literary celebrity is in the description by Dickens in *Little Dorrit* of its inhabitants, the Plornish family and the rest of the Bleeding Hearters. The yard must have been rebuilt shortly afterwards, for it is now a place of Victorian warehouses, split up into multi-occupation by a variety of firms. Moreover, Dickens describes the flight of steps which led down into the yard (but it is now, although paved with old granite setts, on a level with surrounding streets) and a low gateway by which one got out of the yard – all gone, but the yard retains an interest and an atmosphere quite its own.

51

16

17, Red Lion Square

SUPERFICIALLY, THERE is not much to warrant a pilgrimage to Red Lion Square. Its grass and trees certainly form a welcome relief from the acres of brick and stone found in that part of Holborn, but its architecture – Edwardian, 1930s and postwar – is distinctly uninspiring, and I cannot think that the bronze head of Bertrand Russell in the gardens adds much to one's enjoyment of life. Only four old houses, Nos 17, 16, 15 and 14, remain, and nor are these of special quality. Yet No 17, retaining still its original bellpulls and footscraper, housed some of the most extraordinary men in the history of English art and literature. The L.C.C. tablet of 1911 understates the case. It reads, 'In this house lived in 1851 Dante Gabriel Rossetti, Poet and Painter, and from 1856 to 1859 William Morris, Poet and Artist, and Sir Edward C. Burne Jones, Painter'. It omits mention of Walter Deverell, Rossetti's co-tenant of the three rooms on the first floor at £1 a week, and that most enigmatic and tragic figure of the entire Pre-Raphaelite story, Elizabeth Siddall, Deverell's model and eventually Rossetti's wife. Nor does the information hint of other fantastic figures who came there – William Allingham, whose creepy *Maids of Elfen Mere* found a true compliment in Rossetti's early illustration of it, or Jane Burden, later Morris's wife, herself swept up into the charmed circle.

Pre-Raphaelitism had this most remarkable quality, surely unthought of by its founders, that it not only (after initial hostility) made contemporary art appear incredibly stuffy and outdated, at the same time as lifting weaker artists out of their mediocrity, touching them with its emotion and mystic vitality, but it also attracted famous men like Ruskin and unknown women like Lizzie Siddall into its vortex and changed irrevocably their lives. Elizabeth Siddall, the first of the many 'stunners' of the Pre-Raphaelite circle, the emotional, grey-green-eyed girl with the copper-coloured hair and consumptive disposition, remains in spite of the many portraits and descriptions of her somehow unreal and remote, though her end by an overdose of laundanum, to which she was addicted – accidental death was the verdict at the inquest – was real enough. Her

17, Red Lion Square

drawings, though watered-down variants of Rossetti's style of the 1860s, are yet strangely disturbing and compelling. They had enough merit to gain Ruskin's praise and purchase, but they leave one with lowered spirits. This friendship with Ruskin and his introduction of her to his famous friends (Acland and Lewis Carroll among them) at Oxford, to say nothing of her feverish life with Rossetti, all began with the 'discovery' – acting on a hint by Allingham, who had met her first – of Lizzie Siddall working in the bonnet shop in Cranbourn Alley, now a nondescript passage off Leicester Square. She did not begin to pose for Rossetti until he and Deverell moved into Red Lion Square. She had, I feel certain, very special feelings for the handsome young Deverell, but nothing came of them, and then his early death from consumption made Rossetti's monopoly inevitable. Lizzie believed No 17 to be haunted. If not then, it must be so now, at least by memories powerful and intense enough to burst open its prosaic walls. Later in 1856 Rossetti brought his new, idolising young friends from Oxford, William Morris, as yet in the office of Street, the Gothic Revivalist, but already designing medieval-type furniture, and Burne-Jones, 'one of the nicest fellows in dreamland', who, with Rossetti, added paintings to the early Morris furniture, later to be installed in the Red House.

The environment had a tonic effect on both. Within a short time, Burne-Jones was designing his first windows – the stained glass at Bradfield School, crude in colour but already mature in style; the second phase of the Pre-Raphaelite movement was in being. Intense, flame-like emotions, stunners with golden hair, chloral, laundanum, Lizzie's grave at Highgate opened at night and the ms. book of grave-stained poems retrieved –

'I met a lady in the wood
Most beautiful, a fairy's child!'

17
The Last of the Old Bedford

THE LONG-STANDING gap in Camden High Street now filled by an office block for the Abbey National covers the historic site of the Old Bedford. Even so, the Bedford has not quite gone. A substantial part of the auditorium wall remains in the side alley and a bricked-up door with the words 'Exit Only'. I have reason to remember this door; it is the only one I have ever been kicked out of. We used to go up to the Bedford night after night at the Slade – in the Gods, all we could afford. There were still enough old stars to make up, or at least top, a reasonable music-hall bill – George Robey, G. H. Elliott, Nellie Wallace and others of vintage character. One night there was a conjuror on the bill, and one of his illusions was to cast a rod and line into the audience and hook a struggling goldfish. (An extra large float was used, containing water, in which the poor creature was hidden.) I was so filled with hatred and anger that I at once got up and bawled, 'Bloody cruelty, bloody rotten cruelty', and appealed to the audience to join me in throwing the magician off the stage. Were one not fully convinced of the extent of human evil towards animals, one would be stupefied at the barbarism which could subject so inoffensive a creature to such treatment. But the low-voltage audience were not only insensible, but also immobile. Occupied with living up to the fatal English motto, 'Don't look and it will go away', they displayed nothing but inertia. The chucker-out, however, showed more animation, and I found myself hauled out of my seat and given the bum's rush down the gallery stairs and out into the alley through the door marked 'Exit only'. It is possible, of course, that the flapping fish was a dummy merely, in which case there were two dummies – myself and the simulated goldfish – but legerdemain or not, I was jockeyed outdoors.

On happier occasions, I would go up in the mornings, backstage at rehearsals, drawing and chatting up the chorus girls – oldish girls, too, some of them, having seen over-much of Sunday travel in the provinces and theatrical digs. They were compulsives and could live in no other way. There was a good-natured camaraderie among them that has been given permanent form in *The Good Companions.*

Gradually the quality declined, though the Bedford never descended to the smutty revues of the *Eves without Leaves* type that served for Collins's on Islington Green. Eventually, the deserted music hall became a nightly refuge for tramps, and I went there for a period, making drawings in advance of its demolition. A spooky undertaking, for, though there was no tradition of the place being haunted, I did think of Crippen's murdered wife, who was a bottom of the bill turn there. Moreover there are more sympathetic spots to be in than the interior of an abandoned music hall, with the rain beating in through a great hole in the rococo ceiling and a moaning wind opening and shutting doors in a way altogether nerve racking.

The nymphs that held up the plaster draperies of the stage boxes had developed holes in their legs and thighs, showing their essential hollowness; one had entirely lost her head (in common with many other nymphs in and out of the theatre). The whole desolate scene contrasted forcibly with what must have been the Bedford's peak of gaiety – Marie Lloyd's fiftieth birthday held on that same stage (it was her favourite music hall) in Feburary 1920. She had, of course, played at both Bedfords – the first built in 1861 and destroyed by fire in 1899 and the second and last, designed by Bertie Crewe at the turn of the century: Sickert had painted both. The contrast between its nights of gladness and what was before me was emphasised in an eerie way by the masks of comedy below the boxes. Elsewhere the ravaging damp was destroying all the delicate fibrous plasterwork. The masks alone remained undamaged, smiling to themselves, though there was absolutely nothing left at which to be amused.

18
Shoreditch

THAT SHOREDITCH has hardly achieved riches – despite the optimistic note of its church bells in the nursery rhyme – may be why it still has on offer a range of old-style London experiences, curative to those suffering from a surfeit of colour-supplement life styles and trend setting, to all who cannot rhapsodise over developers and progressives. The hub of it, a mid-eighteenth-century church by the elder Dance, St Leonard's, beautifully reconditioned and cleaned, can easily be reached by a No 6 bus from Fleet Street. The churchyard garden comes as a surprise to those unaware of how gratefully the country likes to domicile in town, for here are deep rich grass, well-grown roses, brilliant geraniums and fine old plane trees for the summer heat, and this and the small eighteenth-century house at the entrance to the churchyard and the parish stocks still preserved there are all in surprising and piquant contrast to the thundering great lorries outside. A garden here is fit and proper, for the sermon preached to the Worshipful Company of Gardeners was an annual event here until the last few years, when traffic problems and other considerations occasioned a move to St Giles Cripplegate.

Adjoining the church is one of the few remaining London coffee stalls, where, consuming refreshment, you may contemplate the Shoreditch belles in their progression through dreamy daftness, pregnancy and pram pushing into the regular London ma and finally the pensioner, yclept Senior Citizen. Hoxton Square, Victorian industrialised and therefore entirely delightful to me, is another place of sheltering, friendly planes, and if these are not good enough, why, there is even a great and ancient mulberry at the back of the Children's Hospital along the Hackney Road. Hoxton Street has had an influx of dreary contemporary flats of the kind that have utterly ruined Lambeth Walk, but fortunately a good deal of the old, shabby property remains, and something, too, of the pre-war or even pre-Great War life that should go with it. You can buy acidulous, vivid pickles and cabbage, fit to take the lining off your stomach, appreciate the pigeons' brinkmanship with the local cats, enter easily into conversation with people, eat at the fish bar or study the Victorian tiled pictures in 'The Macbeth' public house.

St Leonard's is an actors' church, with theatrical associations going back to the reigns of Elizabeth and James. Players not only from the two local theatres, 'The Curtain' in Curtain Road and 'The Theatre' in Holywell Lane, but also from 'The Blackfriars' and 'The Globe' chose to live and eventually to be buried in Shoreditch parish. 'The Theatre' in Holywell Lane was built on the site of a nunnery suppressed at the Dissolution, and close to it was the home of Shakespeare's friend, Richard Burbage. The two Shoreditch theatres, playing before Shakespeare came to town, have disappeared without trace; like these our actors, an insubstantial pageant faded, leaving not a rack behind.

Bollard with horseshoes and cannon shield, Woolwich

19

Winchester Palace

N EXTRA pleasure awaits visitors to Bankside nowadays, created by the excavation in 1987 of the foundations of the Great Hall of Winchester Palace. The work consisted of making good the three foundation walls of the undercroft revealed by the demolition of the old flour warehouse which formerly covered the site. The face work and core work in Kentish Rag was carried out by two expert masons brought in from Rochester Castle. Even so, only part of the undercroft has been exposed; the remainder continues under the modern pavements some seventy-five feet eastwards towards Southwark Cathedral. Though mutilated, the rose window is one of the finest of the Decorated period in England; the stone, undoubtedly imported from Northern France (a common practice in the Middle Ages), has been treated to resist further erosion.

Winchester Palace, later Winchester House, was one of the several London residences of medieval bishops. Peterborough Court in Fleet Street commemorates another. Of all these, the only substantial remains are those of the former chapel of Ely Place, Holborn. Winchester Palace was begun early in the twelfth century by Walter Giffard, Bishop of Winchester. Hollar's view of the 1660s shows it as a stately affair, rather like an Oxford College, with enclosed garden quadrangles and an extensive park, for these wordly prelates seldom blushed at ostentation, and expected a splendour of equipage unknown to their Master. Park Street nearby is a reminder of the Bishop's Park. Cardinal Beaufort lived here in the fifteenth century, and it was during his episcopate that the splendid marriage feast of James I of Scotland and Lady Joan Somerset was held in this great hall.

Later, the palace was used as tenements and warehouses, and much of it destroyed. Shakespeare assuredly knew the Palace well. His 'wooden O', 'The Globe', adjoined the bishop's grounds, on a position not precisely known, but somewhere on the brewery site now developed. The failure to locate the whereabouts of 'The Globe' in recent 'digs' is accounted for by the mystery which surrounds the site of Glove Alley. His gibe at the 'Winchester geese' refers

The remains of Winchester Palace

to the prostitutes of Bankside, who traded in some twenty licensed bordellos or stews, leased from the bishops by various brothel keepers, until Henry VIII cleared them out.

Always an optimist on archaelogical sites, I examined the palace foundations with exemplary care, but I found nothing – not even a gold ducat!

To those who remember these riverside ways before the revamping, the entire aspect seems almost to lack conviction. Everything, like Kansas City, is up to date, self-assured, fit for executives and those who are going places in a big way. Broken-down drainpipes to which ferns and buddleia clung, eyeless windows and moribund brickwork have entirely retreated before the transformation. So, too, have the people, though they were rarely encountered, who inhabited those run-down alleys. The shambling figures, cloth capped and in overalls, have been replaced by business men, leggy girls, camera fiends and trend setters to a degree quite unimaginable. You can buy Lazzaroni's biscuits and Italian wine at an up to the minute shop just across the alley from the palace ruins.

Only small areas remain as yet unredeemed – Stoney Street, for example (*Frontispiece*), itself on the site of the palace precincts and leading to Winchester Walk. Sooner or later, its Piranesi-like character, dramatic yet lowering, must give way to upgrading and redevelopment: see it while time permits.

20
Imperial London

I GOT to thinking about the architectural remains of Imperial London through picking up two books. The first, of a size, weight and splendour impossible today, was the *Daily Telegraph Victory Atlas*, circa 1920, with maps showing the rapid increase of British posses-sions – and the annihilation of German. The other was *The Wonder Book of Empire* with a cover showing a majestic Britannia wearing a helmet that makes Pallas Athene's look like a coal scuttle. I have always been in two minds about the Empire, possibly because when I once asked my father what he remembered chiefly about the British Empire Exhibition, he replied, 'Acres of bottled fruit and a drunken Scotsman at Euston carrying a marble clock'.

Sometimes I have thought the Empire a transcendental conception, higher than normal human aims; or else, I have wondered whether it was merely a huge folly – like Beckford's Fonthill Abbey – run up in feverish haste, and certainly in an expansion almost uncanny, out of materials pinched from others: most probably it was both. Anyhow, its evaporation left a strange deposit of architecture behind it: Georgian churches, residences, Chelsea-like streets in all those areas coloured red in the Victory Atlas, and later the Gothic Revival churches transported, as if by a magic carpet, from Dorking to Bengal.

Of this uneasy Indian summer, there is a fantastic memorial in Victoria Street – the 1895 red brick gothic Artillery Mansions, grouped round a mosaic courtyard, where goldfish swim among cast-iron bulrushes in the fountain basin. Here came ex-colonels to languish in Westminster instead of Cheltenham or Eastbourne; civil servants worn out by climate and by administering stern justice and the Pax Britannica. They brought with them camphorwood furniture, brassware and photographs of the Towers of Silence and the Calcutta Ladies' Croquet Club. Wandering there, I wonder if the Empire will become fashionable again, like neglected artists resuscitated by dealers. But I doubt it.

The statue of Queen Victoria opposite the palace – with a hint of genteel vulgarity about it that Kipling's Recessional seems to caution against – always seems to me to sum up Empire splendours. Most statues of the immensely

Capital on the Porter's Rest, Piccadilly

successful queen do this, except for the little known and quite charming one –
the only statue in London of the young queen – once at Lincoln's Inn. Then
there are the former Colonial Offices and the Admiralty Arch, the latter named
once again having that curiously genteel bombast about it, which is so marked a
characteristic of Edwardian public architecture and, indeed, of the period
generally.

   The tower of the Imperial Institute is, I think, very melancholy, being no more
than a lighthouse from which the ocean has receded. Last in an abbreviated
catalogue is another, though less famous, relic of the Empire. This is the former
HQ of the Artists' Rifles behind St Pancras Church. The corps, founded by
artists such as Millais and Leighton, dates from the 1850s and the building from

1888. Here came the artists as the guns of August spoke in the early weeks of the Great War – leaving their colours to join the Colours, so to say. I was thinking of the men who, having passed the portal with its double heads of Minerva in peace and war, never returned, when a woman said to me, 'This is now London's most experimental theatre – Shaw – a rag, a bone and a hank of hair, all that. You follow me?'

Timber of the Roman wharf, St Magnus the Martyr, Billingsgate

21
Strand on the Green

WENT down to Kew in lilac time – a slightly sentimental proceeding perhaps, but why not? – on the way to Strand on the Green, on a day of bright sun and thundercloud, and surveyed from the top of a bus the signs of early summer in London: wisteria out on old garden walls; cow parsley, lime green and of Pre-Raphaelite distinctness in the shadows of the grass; sheep safely grazing in the buttercup meadows at Ham; chestnuts fully out at Kew – and certainly the lilac; and on the bus, groovy schoolgirls pulling out packets of gaspers and emitting clouds of smoke like unswept chimneys. The view of Strand on the Green as I leaned over the parapet of Kew Bridge was altogether delightful, for then one's back is turned to the horrid, towering blocks of flats that disgrace the skyline upstream. The tide was on the turn, and the sunlight played fitfully, now here, now there, on the long curving strip of Georgian houses and cottages. A pleasure boat came chugging up from Kingston, with a cargo of kids waving like mad. On such a day, the railway bridge, drab enough at other times, takes on pictorial qualities – so much so that on summer afternoons when there is a skiff or two on the river and glancing brilliant lights on the water, the whole arrangement becomes a subject that Monet would have sat down to paint. But why Strand on the Green? What Green? The Strand is there right enough, this being the somewhat muddy beach of the Middlesex foreshore, below the causeway dotted with willows and enriched by river-loving weeds. Still, there is no evidence of a green, unless the name can be held to refer to Kew Green across the river. But hardly, and the only other possibility I can see is that in the days when King Edward VII, as Prince of Wales, used to take Chiswick House for occasional use in the summers of a century ago, the Green was the area of land immediately behind the riverside fringe, now built over with Victorian terraces of fierce brick and tiled porch, in complete contrast to the almost stately Georgian houses and charming cottages of the waterside with their walls covered by wisteria and *Clematis montana*.

The painter Zoffany lived here in one of the finest of the eighteenth-century houses, suitably marked with a plaque: artists, in common with doctors and

Strand on the Green

solicitors, have a way of housing themselves agreeably. Zoffany's fame brought the fashionables – the gentry and the quality – to this then fishing and boat-building village to be painted in those superb conversation pieces at which he was unrivalled. Like many other artists – Hogarth, for example – Zoffany was not content with what he could do uniquely, effortlessly, but had ambitions towards the grand style, and to that end used local characters as models for the disciples in an altarpiece of the Last Supper.

Until recently Strand on the Green had four pubs – surely a generous helping for such a short stretch, especially as there are others at each end of Kew Bridge. The pubs were the Victorian 'Steam Packet', now transformed into 'The Dôme Café Bar' and the three that remain – 'The Bell and Crown', 'The City Barge' and, lastly, almost opposite the tree-shaded eyot which divides the river, 'The Bull's Head' with a seventeenth-century exterior and a mostly Edwardian interior. Cromwell is believed to have held a Council of War here; it is not unlikely as there was fighting around here in the neighbourhood of Turnham Green. At any rate, one may hope that the excellence of its fare and its general comfort softened somewhat the asperity of his Ironsides. It is all very English, Strand on the Green, but a little like Venice, too, especially if you go there when the winter tides are lapping the garden walls and swans and Chinese geese are cruising about unconcernedly, close to the houses, unaware, apparently, of a rise in their affairs.

Much as I admire this fringe of charming houses, I could not live there myself, satisfying as it is to watch the lazy life of the river and study the birds among the willows, for Strand on the Green has become a great tourist attraction during the summer months. The pubs and 'The Dôme Café Bar' are packed tight, and a continuous parade of rubbernecks files along the waterfront path under the houses. These strollers have a habit of staring into the lower rooms of the houses in a way quite exasperating. If I lived there, I should empty the slops over them, as used to be done in old Edinburgh – without the warning, *'Gardez l'eau.'*

22

Barnard's Inn, Holborn

HE ENGLISH, long practised in the art of swift adaptation to altered circumstances, are also adept at converting their buildings as the trade winds might require. We have been doing this since the Reformation, when we turned the superannuated abbeys and churches into stables and cowsheds. London is full of examples: a staggering one was a proposal to turn St Mark's, North Audley Street, into a bazaar – money changing in the Temple, if you like.

Another, not nearly so depressing, is the recent use of the old hall of Barnard's Inn for a restaurant. It was not the first old hall to go in for catering: Crosby Hall, now removed to Chelsea, was one of Frederick Gordon's first successful ventures as a restaurateur. If you want to find Barnard's Inn, you must go down a white-tiled passage in Holborn Bars, immediately opposite the Prudential Offices, through an iron gate below the sculptured device of the Mercers' Company – a crowned maiden and the motto *'Honor Deo'* – and so into an irregular yard, once lined with trees. Of the once extensive Inn, an Inn of Chancery attached to Gray's Inn, only the tiny hall, probably of the late fifteenth century, remains, but with its ancient timberwork and lantern, it is yet a delightful bit of old London. Some Georgian additions are there also, flanking the hall. For the rest, the remaining buildings of Barnard's Inn are late Victorian, used as offices and now vacant.

The old hall, a listed building, came into the possession of the Mercers' Company in 1891, and was used as the dining-room of the Mercers' School until a couple of decades ago. The Prudential took a lease in 1961 of various buildings in Barnard's Inn, including the old school hall, but vacated most of its accommodation there during the early 1970s. Then the ancient hall was let to Melbourne Hart and Company, the cigar importers, who used it as a cigar store, perhaps the most worthy use to which the hall has been put since it was built as the town residence of the Dean of Lincoln in the reign of Henry VI. He, poor chap, left his hall to his Cathedral Chapter, so that prayers might there be said for his soul, but the lawyers were there very soon afterwards. I feel sure that the

Dean, if he failed to get the prayers, would not be adverse to the cigars in the coming time, though he might well jib at the ubiquitous, sometimes succulent pizza.

Today, however, the old hall, empty and forlorn, is at the centre of redevelopment plans. In the courtyard on my last visit in the late autumn of 1988 were the remains of an archaeological dig, weed grown, waterlogged, depressing: all I could see of interest were a few courses at medieval level of a wall of rough hewn stone, bits of tiles and a few old bones – not, one hopes, bones of contention.

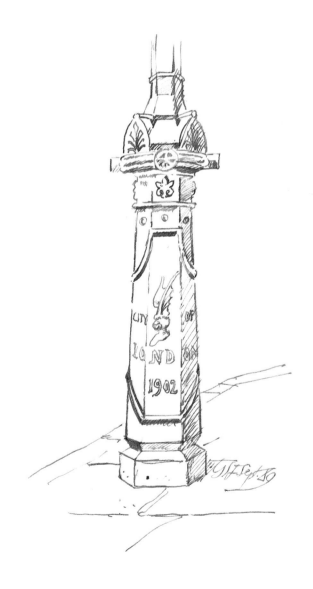

City of London lamp standard, Frederick's Place

23

An Islington Perambulator

YOU NEED to understand how Islington came to be what it is to fully appreciate it. When I first knew it and went up in the gallery at Collins's to an evening's music hall for a bob, it was recognisably still in the late Victorian working-class phase painted by Sickert – a place of dingy areas and ha'porths of this and that, where the aspidistra was kept flying in lace-curtained windows and where today's Islington features – poodles and bottles of wine – were as rare as fur coats in Hell. But it is this modification to a basically working-class structure that gives the area, especially its older markets, such fascination. The three markets – Exmouth Street in Finsbury, Chapel Street and Camden Passage – are so rich as to require continual study, but the London connoisseur can give them a sufficient curtain raiser in a long Saturday, with satisfaction guaranteed.

Camden Passage in my Collins period was entirely unknown to fame. All the shops from the beginning at what is now the Pierrepont Arcade to the doll's hospital at the end were aboriginal. A few were just junk shops that sold for an old song the flat irons, oil lamps and Staffordshire groups that Grandma had chucked out. On the site of the Pierrepont Arcade was a dilapidated terrace called Paradise Row, inhabited by indigent Irish; Repuke's still provided horse-drawn funerals, and not a tourist was in sight.

Since then all has changed, and the whole area has become a sort of Greenwich Village, devoted to flogging the second-hand. I regret the loss of character, but it is all very entertaining. Prices vary from the possible to the impossible. Not long ago I picked up a fine Phil May drawing of Volendam for only £13, but generally prices incline to be stiffish and often just plain daft. The shops and some of the stalls tend to specialise, but on the whole the stuff is miscellaneous, and repays a careful picking over, especially among the collection of open air stalls at the top of Charlton Place.

The latest development is the kerbside outfit, and this you will find around Camden Head public house. At first there were only a few sellers out of suitcases, but now there is a constellation of them, and stalls, too, for the greater capitalists

Old shops, Newington Green

– even the windowsills of the pub are used for the display of junk. You can find anything inorganic that the human heart has ever coveted – old Ewbanks, bashed up dolls and toys, plaster busts of the Army Club cigarette staff officer ('£17, sir, and it's genuine Royal Doulton'), books; there are souvenirs of the Festival of Britain, very dreary and pathetic, moth-eaten stuffed birds, ditto, faded photographs and sunshades that would have distressed Madame Butterfly more than Pinkerton did. There is even a framed dog licence of 1927 – somebody's former chum – and this I find the most mournful by far. One old man has nothing to sell but a blue jerry filled with soil and a gasping plant – the whole being either a throwback to Victorian London or a subtle surrealist happening – one cannot be sure which.

Beyond the pub and in front of the warehouse, now converted and rechristened 'The Georgian Village' is another group of stalls. Here are some specialists dealing in old iron or brasswork, bottles, vintage kitchen equipment and *art deco* objects once sold by F. W. Woolworth in his nothing-over-sixpence epoch. Saturday is the best day, though the market is also open on Wednesday, but only until about two o'clock. These dealers are very sharp up to the mark. Most of them know the exact value of their wares: if you find a real bargain, you will deserve the George Cross. Many of them, anyway, sell to each other, particularly where specialities are concerned, such as model steam engines, military histories or medals. The whole of the street from the snazzy Royal Bank of Scotland block up to Islington Green has so turned its back on its gasping down-at-heels past that a local Rip van Winkle would be totally disorientated and discomfited. Expensive restaurants have replaced Lou's old clo' shop and Levy's gramophone emporium, and you can buy pub mirrors, rocking horses and *art nouveau* busts in the places where earlier customers could hardly afford a packet of Woodbines. A million years ago, in the 1950s, there used to shamble along the passage a poor ancient derelict, singing (as a message on his battered old hat advertised) 'Songs of Caruso'. Also in those prehistoric times, there was an old girl at the end of the passage who ran a dolls' hospital and toyshop where Kate Carney bought a toy horse for the then unknown Charlie Chaplin, appearing at Collins's low down on the bill.

In brighter Islington, an immense effort is required to believe that such things ever were or could be. Yet despite intensive up-grading, considerable fragments of the old village of Islington remain: eighteenth and nineteenth-century properties that appear in the High Street above the shops that have been unceremoniously jammed in below. I illustrate a characteristic example of this on Newington Green, a pair of picturesque brick-pilastered houses dating from 1658.

24

The London That Never Was

Y WEBSTER'S dictionary succinctly defines a myth as 'a story invented as a veiled explanation of a truth'. So it is; there is always a factual nucleus, however microscopic, in the nature myths that fictively describe natural events or the culture myths woven round a hero, like those of our own Arthurian cycle. We might more properly call these London fables 'myth conceptions' or, in other words, moonshine. All historic cities have them: Mantua has the house of Rigoletto, though the jester never lived; there is at least a big question mark over Juliet's house in Verona; and London has a dismaying collection that no amount of critical exposure will ever dislodge. One of my *bêtes noires* (shared by all Dickensians) is the charming old shop in Portsmouth Street which luckily escaped the ravages of the Clare Market demolitions at the beginning of the century. It calls itself 'The Old Curiosity Shop' and attracts coach loads of Americans, yet it has nothing whatever to do with Dickens. It was merely dubbed that by a Mr Tessyman who occupied the premises between 1868 and 1877, merely because of his business as a dealer in books and prints: the imaginative 'immortalised by Charles Dickens' came later, and has stuck fast. Dickens, himself, is on record as having localised the house as being No 10 Green Street, near Leicester Square – now entirely demolished. Dickens's grandson wrote in 1902, 'Among the places which have gained a false sanctity is the Old Curiosity Shop in Portsmouth Street.' The clinching evidence is contained in the first edition of the book with wood-engraved illustrations by G. Cattemole. That Dickens exercised a close control on his illustrators is well known: he was constant in pointing out incongruities for their attention. Cattemole's illustration to the close of Chapter 12 is therefore incontrovertible. Nell and her grandfather are setting out on the journey, leaving a narrow street of typical eighteenth-century London houses with the Curiosity Shop to the right – a plain Georgian house with a projecting, two-columned porch, against which are leaning bits of panelling and a carved figure.

Rumours of demolitions (I hope unfounded) round Cardinal Cap Alley,

Bankside, remind me of another London house that will not stand up to cross-examination – the old house next to the alley which announces itself as being the home of Sir Christopher Wren and also, if possible, more outrageously the lodging of Catherine of Aragon. This particular piece of conjecture is really too nonsensical to bother gainsaying. First, Wren's addresses – Idol Lane, St James's and Hampton Court among them – are well known. Second, as one of the most eminent men of the period, he would never have lived among the cruel bear and bull baitings, the brothels and the ruffians and blackguards of Bankside as it was then. Third, the house was built in the early nineteenth century. What happened was that an old sea-captain some decades ago, having heard that Wren watched the building of St Paul's through a telescope (itself a piece of moonshine), decided that he must therefore have watched it from the house in Cardinal's Wharf. Yet, by a mischievous combination of adverse planets, this deception insinuated itself into my own work. I once scripted a London film, excellently produced for the most part and starring James Mason, but my material ran short of screening time by a minute or two. On seeing the private showing, I found to my dismay that a sequence of the 'Wren' house had been added by the film makers to take up the extra time – there it was, the old hydra-headed, impossible-to-kill legend again, and this time flourishing under my own name, as large as life and twice as inconvenient. But what is true is that Axel Munthe, author of the immortal *Story of San Michele* and a lover of Bankside, bought the house as a wedding present for his son, Major Malcolm Munthe, after the 1939 –45 war.

I once unwittingly put such a groundless story into circulation when I moved into the old house on the river at 59, Rotherhithe St. At that time I was charmed with Dickens's description of Solomon Gills's 'The Little Midshipman' in the Minories, so I christened my own house – not a ships' instrument maker's but definitely riparian – 'The Little Midshipman', and had it written up in Roman lettering, finely done. Almost immediately, the river-boat guides were informing their rubbernecked passengers that there was 'Dickens's original "Little Midshipman" from *Dombey and Son*'.

Here, then, is a nosegay of London weeds. There are others. There is no documentary proof, for instance, that Rahere, founder of the Priory of St Bartholomew in Smithfield, was ever a jester. And Dick Whittington – at least the story of Bow Bells and the cat – might turn out to be nothing more than a pantomime part of the London that Never Was.

25

Return of a Cockle Shed Hero

OSTERS ADVERTISING the Leigh Regatta and cruises on old paddle-steamers from Southend Pier reminded me, on a hot autumn morning, that a day out at Leigh-on-Sea was overdue. Some years since when I had hospitable relatives in Leigh, I used to go there often, an essential item being several state visits to the cockle sheds. We would go for cockles even on bitter Boxing Day mornings, accompanied by my Cairn terrier who always had a little saucerful to himself. I christened us the Cockle Shed Heroes.

From early times, through the Middle Ages and up to the coming of the railway (to Leigh in 1854 and to Southend, London's other watering place, in 1856), Leigh was almost entirely confined to the waterfront, with a few houses up hill and others round the church. Most of the present-day Leigh dates from the 1890s onwards, and is of no interest whatever. Old Leigh is all important. At the rear of the new station, built in 1933 (the old one survives as the HQ of the Yacht Club), is a vast car park. To it, from five o'clock onwards, pour streams of London commuters, stale from the City. Others at once head for Cockle Row for a plate of shell fish, throwing off the pointlessness of the day in the sea air, whilst viewing the evening light glancing on the water and on sails and cloud banks far away. After that journey through the badlands from Fenchurch Street – nightmare blocks of flats, greasy parking lots, industrial sites – Bromley by Bow, Barking, 1930s Dagenham and dreadful Basildon – horror almost all the way to the castle and cornfields at Hadleigh – their view of estuary and plate of humble cockles is thoroughly well deserved.

The strip of the Thames estuary from Hadleigh to Sheerness is, I believe, one of the most stimulating and satisfying anywhere, only rivalled by the Lancashire coast from Lytham to Fleetwood for compacted interest and variety. I try not to believe that providence caused the Thames estuary to be prolific of shell fish in order that Londoners could have bread and butter and cockle teas at Leigh, though the evidence strongly suggests this. But I cannot believe that the Deity created those elegant ribbed shells with a secondary intention of their being shovelled

Cockle sheds, Leigh-on-sea

up, after the inhabitants have been eaten, by the ton from the Leigh beaches – nowadays a minor Leigh industry – crushed and used on car parks. However, the succulent bivalves were esteemed by antique nations; I have seen the shells of the Leigh cockles, once eaten by Roman legionaries, at Roman level in the Cornhill area; and I have found cockle shells (but not, of course, from Leigh) in quantities in the top soil of Troy.

Old Leigh, I find, hasn't changed much. A few old houses have gone, one at a time, since the war, perhaps the most regrettable being the two Elizabethan cottages, timber framed, plastered and with a deep overhang, known as Juniper's shop, which went in the 1950s, but on the whole impious hands have left it alone. A handful of small houses have appeared on an old empty site in the High Street and some of the cockle sheds have been either enlarged or partly rebuilt, but somehow Leigh appears resistant to change, and happily there are increasing numbers of connoisseurs who are fully aware of its unique character.

The August morning was as roasting as if in Italy. The tide was out, the intense glare of the sunlight turning the mud flats into a dazzling pale blue, in harmony with the verditer blue with which most of Leigh's fishing boats are painted. Even the gulls found the heat oppressive and contented themselves with sitting at ease in the shallows. Leigh is a place for lotus eaters as well as shell fish eaters; loafers seemed mesmerised by the heat, the boats and the incoming tide. Crusoe-like figures apparently made of flexible bronze did something with ropes or brushes here and there on the beach and on the boats; dogs made sudden mad investigations, and young men stripped to the waist shovelled up cockle shells or unloaded them from dredgers just off shore, but it was all very lax in the noonday sun. I made an excellent lunch – I had it in mind all along – from cockles, buttered rolls and tea, in company with dozens of other happy-go-luckies in open-necked shirts, print dresses and dreadful slacks: the kind of people who propagate themselves without variation from one generation to another, who go to Blackpool, Margate, Southend and who win wars, consume ices and eat cockles washed down with tea or Tizer.

Leigh's sandy beach – the other being nothing but cockle shells – at Bell's Wharf was so densely packed that you could not hope to get a stick of rock between the Cockneys. Middle-aged women with years of nagging behind them were saturating themselves in Mills and Boon; sharpish younger specimens barked orders at their kids; youths displayed anatomies as browned off as if tanned on the Venetian Lido and the children gambolled in the waves. . . . A thought more self-conscious is Old Leigh, but definitely not spoiled.

26
Around Sadler's Wells

WHENEVER I find myself near Sadler's Wells, I involuntarily think of a charming spot in Lancashire, Lytham St Anne's. I used to visit one of the last of the old shrimp women there in her pretty cottage in Westby Street with snapdragons growing from the whitewashed backyard walls. Old Sarah's daughter presented me with something I coveted, a Victorian doorstep of Joe Grimaldi, complete with gin barrel, sausages and his catchwords (Grimaldi was the first to use them), 'Don't you tell', on the base.

Sadler's Wells, originally a holy well, was rediscovered and developed as a spa and pleasure garden by Mr Sadler. In time, a threatre was added – the springs are still in existence under it – and here Grimaldi, most illustrious of all those who have tumbled in sawdust rings or appeared in pantomime, acquired his fame. He was subject to fits of intense nervous melancholy, and once, when driven to consulting a specialist for relief, was advised to go and see Grimaldi as a therapy, to which the patient replied, 'But I *am* Grimaldi.' Many amusing and some tragic accounts of this sort can be found in *The Life of Joseph Grimaldi*, ghosted by Dickens from material gathered by his father, John Dickens – an admirable accompaniment to wandering in the area.

My favourite approach is northwards from St James's Walk behind Clerkenwell Church through streets of well-proportioned terraces. Fine doors and balconies occur here and there, but the quarter has a somewhat crestfallen air, as if it knew it belonged properly to Bloomsbury, but had got itself dislocated and unfashionable through an error of judgement. Halfway to Sadler's Wells, one crosses the end of Exmouth Market with the pub, 'The London Spa', marking the site of yet another and minor spa at the corner. There is a rich effect to be had here on a bright winter day – a purely Italian composition – for sunlight strikes directly down the market, picking out colour on stalls, vegetables and greenery in pots; the familiar London figures and their dogs are gilt edged, momentarily transformed by the prismatic light, against which, at the far end, is a dark mass, the campanile of the Holy Redeemer.

Alongside the theatre is Arlington Way, a charming street of small Georgian terraced houses with shops below, mostly original – No 23 being entirely so. There is a card shop, a bookshop and a genuine old-fashioned mixed grocery and sweetshop with bottles of cough candy, pear drops and wine gums in the window, just as it should be. There is also a curious old stable yard with grass-grown cobbles and hollyhocks, a relic of the days of donkey and pony carts, and a choice half-pint-size pub, 'The Harlequin', with a theatrical flavour resulting from pictures of ballerinas and lithographed song sheets of the Victorian Lion Comique, 'The Great Vance', rival of the affections of pit and gallery to Champagne Charlie. Where Arlington Way joins Chadwell Street is a new four-storeyed block with its main elevation on St John Street: it is in the Georgian style and of remarkable quality – remarkable for its brickwork, proportions and general finish – and is an example of what can be done when a civilised scheme to harmonise with existing work takes precedence over an ambition to create something new and exciting, of which we have already had more than enough. The anthemion or Greek honeysuckle balconies are good copies of the old ones in Chadwell Street. These came from the pattern book of an early, little-known nineteenth-century architect, L. N. Cottingham, who managed to lay impious hands on several ancient churches, including Rochester Cathedral, in what was optimistically termed restoration. Nonetheless, I believe that his elegant ironwork in north and east London saved him from the Devil.

27

London Courts

PRONOUNCEMENTS BY public men and women usually fail to stir my jaded nerves, so I find; yet the comments by the Prince of Wales on the architectural cruelties that are worked off on us, the unresisting Philistines, could hardly be more valuable! And I was delighted that the *Daily Telegraph* seconded his remarks, for the planners, the developers and the architectural sultans have had it their way long enough – long enough to make the City of London a home-made Manhattan, to convert cities like Birmingham and Manchester into obscenities and defile in some way or other almost all sizeable English towns. Not a cubic foot of this is architecture; it is building merely, building that has no aesthetic qualities, no life-enhancing capacities, monstrous, worthless and without meaning, except, of course, for the ones who are to make money out of it. It is high time that those with a voice, indifferent to being marked down as ossified reactionaries, blew the gaff on the whole movement. In spite of the economic decline, these things still go on, as they did in similar circumstances in the 1930s, simply because suitability is of no account when it becomes a question of squeezing the maximum juice out of a site.

Lancashire Court, a pleasing antique corner off Bond Street, a place of small businesses and cottage-type property, is now a target for a consortium of developers; being elderly, interesting and slightly shabby, the court is, of course, as attractive to capitalists as jam at a picnic to wasps. Two interesting courts are actually within a stone's throw of the controversial National Gallery site – Hobhouse Court and Excel Court, Whitcomb Street. The first named, on Crown property, is an example of what can be done in the way of modernisation when carried out by a sensitive architect with not too much money to spend. The entry leads into a charming courtyard built on the site of the former premises of Fredk Cope, the builders, and the old coachyard behind. Everything that could be retained has been carefully rehabilitated – the warehouses fronting on Whitcomb Street, the Georgian houses on the far (the west) side of the court and a small Regency house on the right-hand side: these with a cobbled pavement, cast-iron

Excel Court, Whitcomb Street

lamp standards and a tree or two add up to a totally satisfactory job. Excel Court, farther along, is a rum little entry. It was once the home of Sir Mortimer Wheeler. Today its most eminent resident is a blackbird, who warbles away the fugitive days of summer. There is an ancient gas lamp still in use (there were two until the Council took one away, but the remaining lamp is still cleaned regularly). There used to be a couple of ancient cast-iron baths, in one of which was a sturdy fig tree (a tree grows in Brooklyn!), undoubtedly – since no human being planted it – grown from a bird-sown seed from one of the National Gallery fig trees. All is now cleaned up, and camellias and hollies form a small and welcome town garden at the far end. There is a little dairy at the corner of the court and Whitcomb Street, which has changed in these last few years since the time when the late Tony Hancock used to prop up the bar of the 'Racquet' pub, but something of the village atmosphere remains, at least for the present.

Other London courts – a handful out of a considerable list – include Friary Court and Ambassadors Court, St James's Palace – a stately pair these – Wine Office Court leading to the Cheshire Cheese, Wash House Court near the Charterhouse and Mitre Court near Ely Place. There are a number linking Maiden Lane with the Strand and others in and around St Martin's Lane (Cecil Court where Arnold Bennett once edited a women's magazine) and Seven Dials. A favourite lounging-place of mine is Wardrobe Court on the south side of Ludgate Hill – virtually a bird sanctuary on summer evenings; a human sanctuary, too, for the peace of the court is such that it is hard to believe, even in working hours, that the stink and grinding of London traffic is only a few yards away.

28
Woolwich

REVISITED WOOLWICH as a guest of the hospitable Artillerymen of the Garrison and took time off round the town. Not everyone possibly shares my enthusiasm for the place: take away the eighteenth-century barracks, the Royal Military Academy and the open spaces owned by the military, and much of the rest would be somewhat grotty! The Mississippi-type ferry boats, on which I used to joy-ride afternoons away, are just a memory; tower blocks, nightmarishly hideous, of the kind that have disfigured most of our unhappy cities, loom up from the town and disrupt the superb barrack façade. Others, like Imhotep's step pyramid, have replaced the early nineteenth-century terraces by the common, where General Gordon lived.

But the curious sensation that Queen Victoria is in the offing remains strong, as it does in all our garrison towns, so that one is not surprised to find her initials with acanthus foliage beautifully cut in brick on the post office wall. Indeed, she watches us by proxy in 'beloved Alex's' portrait in the charming pub windows of 'The Princess of Wales'. The markets are a joy. The covered one – toys, meat, fancy goods, snack bar – reminds me nostalgically of those of my native Lancashire, and has the same old-fashioned, everyday character that is so reassuring in crackpot times like these. The outdoor one in Beresford Square is made doubly interesting by having the early and late nineteenth-century entrance of the Arsenal as a background, whence emerged the famous 'Woolwich Infant' and other pieces of ordnance used by the English in their great days to subdue the heathen and impose the *Pax Britannica*.

The façade of the Barracks is a liberal education in fitness for architectural purpose, in variety harmonised into unity and in immaculate proportions. The architect is unknown, but it was built between 1774 and 1802, when Sir Charles Frederick was Surveyor General. The façade, one of the longest in Europe, was originally the front of a vast parallelogram, with stabling and men's quarters behind. On rising ground on the east side are the ruins of the garrison church, built in 1863 under Herbert's authority in his Wilton Lombardic style and shattered in the last war. The original garrison church, part of the main block, was turned in the 1860s into a garrison theatre, which survived until recent years.

The officers' mess is a magnificent hall, lofty but still intimate, and lined with Royal portraits; dining here one has the feeling that it is almost worthwhile seeking a reputation in the cannon's mouth. The Royal Military Academy, built originally for the 'Gentleman Cadets' in 1805–6, is a charming gingerbread Gothic toy by James Wyatt. Nothing as a constructor or planner and knowing of Gothic mouldings little more than a costermonger, Wyatt, here as at Fonthill, was a superb purveyor of the romantic and picturesque. The centre block now houses the Royal Artillery library and a Royal Artillery museum which is open on weekdays to the public.

Here on the common and parade ground were held the great manoeuvres and military occasions before Aldershot was. Still, a hint of the old glory came to me as I watched a modern Major General step into his helicopter to be borne aloft into golden-edged clouds – like the Virgin in an Italian holy picture....

Water conduit, Market Place, Woolwich

29
The Borough Market

I HAVE FORBODINGS that one day in the not-distant future, Londoners will be told that the Borough Market has become too congested, too outmoded to continue on its present ancient site, and is to be transferred to a more convenient one elsewhere. The auguries are not propitious: the slick new blocks now completed on the waterfront on the site of St Mary Overy's dock and the developments that are replacing the old, worn, dignified warehouses make everything round them seem shabby and inefficient, and there are the obvious difficulties of wheedling the vast container lorries from the Continent into the narrow streets of the market. Hence, another Covent Garden saga seems on the cards: the reluctant departure of the market men, the conversion of the atmospheric old houses of the area, such as the group in Park Street I illustrate, into trendy restaurants, art shops and what-not – in short the unlimited boring nonsense that appalls one now in Convent Garden.

The market, held in the High Street and along London Bridge at the period of Chaucer's Canterbury Tales, was moved to its present site in the eighteenth century and extended in the 1920s. As seen today, it is one of the diminishing number of genuinely atmospheric and interesting quarters of London, and that alone constitutes a danger. There are magnificent sudden views of the cathedral – for example, from the west end of Winchester Walk – all with a market foreground, and this is as it should be but so seldom is in England: a Gothic cathedral should never be encountered in an open space, but should be watched for and found surprisingly at the termination of narrow streets.

Strong odours of over-ripe fruit – bananas, melons, plums – meet the nostrils. Warnings against the dumping of discarded stuff are posted here and there, but the dumps seem as immovable as the cast-iron bollards which are also a notable feature of the area. If you are down on your luck, you can join those who make regular inspections of the piles of superannuated fruit, humans and birds alike, on the offchance of an acceptable grapefruit or a couple of Victorias. Sparrows, blackbirds and pigeons do well here, for not only is food lying around for the picking, but there is free accommodation also in the cast iron and glass canopied

Railway Arches and Park Street, Southwark

market and in the arches of the railway. In the narrow, cobbled alleys, you will find the porter's or coster's barrow still in use, brightly painted in traditional colours of scarlet and green, with the name of the owner lettered in yellow. There are pubs, too, suitably appropriate for the area, 'The Market Porter' and 'The Wheatsheaf' – of course with a special early morning licence – and caffs of just the right kind, the kind for me, that chalk up the menus as the caffs of Les Halles used to do before that was economised away – caffs where you get strong, thick tea and Zeppelins in a cloud – the authentic London, miraculously surviving.

Of course, I may be wrong. Raree shows, souvenirs and synthetic fun may never take over. But

> *'Old experience doth attain*
> *To something like prophetic strain.'*

30
Graveyard Gardens

I GOT TO thinking about the graveyard gardens of London as a result of watching a BBC television dramatisation of Bleak House, showing Jo and Lady Deadlock peering through the gates of a churchyard super-fatted with burials – that of St John, Drury Lane, now a garden playground. There are over forty churchyard gardens in the City alone, and together with those in surrounding areas, such as St Andrew's, Holborn, and St Leonard's, Shoreditch, they form an impressive total of peaceful green spots for lunch-time escapists from grit, petrol and the production of useless paperwork. Postman's Park, the second largest of those in the City and consisting of the joint burial grounds of St Botolph and Christchurch Greyfriars, was opened in the early 1880s, co-incident with the Metropolitan Open Spaces Act which gave an impetus to this turning of churchyards into parks, and it remains very Victorian, which is why I prefer it. The fig trees, the black poplars, the nineteenth-century style carpet bedding, together with the Arts and Crafts tiled memorials to other-wise unsung heroes and heroines who gave their lives in catastrophes on land and sea, give it an unmistakable period quality: so does the light, which comes only from overhead, giving the foliage a curious dark richness even on summer days.

The tiny, wedge-shaped garden of St Mary le Strand – all that is left after the Victorians and Edwardians took off their slices – is to me a wonder – how it remains fresh in that petrol-charged air: its two magnolias are among the earliest to bloom in London. St Leonard's, Shoreditch, has a large garden of admirable quality, and fittingly, for it is there that the Worshipful Company of Gardeners met annually to hear a sermon on the works of God in creation as established by Thomas Fairchild, a famous London gardener at the time of William and Mary. Some of these gardens are mostly pavement, like that of St Peter Westcheap at the corner of Wood Street, with its great plane tree reminding us of Wordsworth's 'Tale of Poor Susan'. Others are very small – a mere slip of turf as in Silver Street or the lawn and seats as at St Mary Staining, both churches having entirely disappeared, or lawn and paved areas as that of St Michael Paternoster Royal.

Many again have something of special historic interest; St Olave, Hart Street, for example, where Pepys and his wife worshipped and are buried: there, the charming garden churchyard is raised above the level of the church, the result of interments during the Plague. Perhaps the most ambitious garden is at St Dunstan's in the east, now quite mature. The tower and spire are Wren's Gothic, undamaged, but the rest of the church by David Laing was reduced to a shell by war-time bombing. It was a fine thought to restore the damaged tracery (I remember Colonel Dove telling me the difficulties he had in finding old masons experienced enough to cut the mouldings) and then to plant out the entire site as a delightful garden. We may hope that the shell of Christchurch Grayfriars will be similarly enhanced.

Whether the Victorians who initiated the churchyard-into-garden movement were quite right in bundling out the dead (however ceremoniously), I have my doubts, but these misgivings, I am sure, are not shared either by the bird population or by the temporary refugees from computers.

Drinking fountain, St Mary, Aldermanbury

31

The Tom Browne Story

N O 7, HARDY Road, Blackheath – undistinguished by a blue plaque – was the last home of a greatly talented artist, Tom Browne, now unjustly undervalued except by the few students of what was once called 'commercial art'. Yet almost everyone knows one example of his work – the Johnie Walker trademark – the Regency buck, beaver hatted and top booted, appraising us through his quizzing glass, as he strides purposefully onwards, presumably to the nearest tumbler of his own whisky. When twinges of homesickness occur to me in foreign parts, I invariably run my eye over the bottles in a bar, and there he is – 'home from home' as the Blackpool landladies used to claim.

Older readers will know Tom Browne by the knockabout characters he created in the halfpenny comic *Chips* – Weary Willie and Tired Tim, whose adventures were featured on its front page from the 1890s until the comic folded in 1953. Tom (like Arthur Mee and D. H. Lawrence) descended on London as an unknown from Nottingham, at first very much as a printers' hack and publishers' dogsbody. He soon managed a foothold in commercial and in more serious art, and was elected a member of the Royal Institute of Painters in Watercolour. His work in both sorts is overdue for the attention of those true resurrection men, the dealers, along with Dudley Hardy, John Hassall and others of his circle and type. The artist (unrelated, incidentally, to Hablot K. Brown ['Phiz'] or Gordon Browne) was somewhat less of a Bohemian than either Hassall or Hardy: in fact he was athletic, a furious cyclist and a dedicated globe trotter, habits which, together with consistent overwork, assisted in killing him at forty.

Some of his most charming watercolours are of Volendam, the Dutch fishing village then on the edge of the Zuyder Zee, a favourite haunt also of Phil May and other artists of that 'Miss Hook of Holland' period: odd how they constellated in fishing towns – Staithes, Whitby, Newlyn, St Ives, Dieppe and Volendam. I thought I had alighted on a Dutch Tom Browne recently in Battersea – as seen from the other side of the road – but it was a reproduction merely: too hopefully,

Tom Browne's house and studio, No 7 Hardy Road, Blackheath

I saw it as a fellow to the one I already have, drawn in Tokyo in 1909, the last year of the artist's life.

Hardy Road, begun in the 1880s, was being built up during the years of Browne's residence, with vacant plots and construction still going on. The houses are a mixture of the aesthetic and the Edwardian periods and even of the 1930s. The road has never been renumbered, though Tom's attractive Edwardian home – more perhaps that of a stockbroker than that of a successful artist – no longer has the name 'Woollaton' he gave to it.

The house in more recent times became the home of John Bratby, whose wife, herself an artist, has told me of the bits and pieces they unearthed of Tom Browne's life there, including, if I remember correctly, a photograph of the artist as a part-time officer in one of the Territorial regiments. Had Tom not been destroyed by cancer in 1910, he might have been rubbed out in the retreat from Mons in 1914 or thereafter.

32
Soho

s I have remarked elsewhere in this book, one runs a risk in today's London – or anywhere else in England for that matter – in mentioning some dusty, half-forgotten corner or an old-established shop: the chances are that, while the volume is yet at the printer's, the whole thing will have been economised off the earth. But in autumn, 1988, the eighteenth-century building of an interesting old shop, dusty and forlorn and closed for a long time, the premises of Benford and O'Shea, watch and clock makers since 1869, remains at the corner of Meard Street. The closure, because of ever-increasing overheads, draws attention to the way Soho is being eroded and changed out of all recognition.

Once everybody knew everybody in a close-knit community in which the village atmosphere was distinct and strong: now the old-established businesses are being pushed out by high rents and increasing numbers of porn merchants and big operators. Meths men and drug addicts are always around. Even the prostitutes have changed. You see them in old photographs draped in platinum fox furs and clutching handbags, propping up the street corners, as frowsy as a revivalist meeting, in the days when Sunday papers regularly ran articles taking the lid off the Soho stews.

The prostitutes were then older women, an acknowledged part of the Soho scene: they used to be good to the children and old folk – the tarts with the golden hearts of French fiction – and go regularly for check-ups at the hospital, now a refuge for drop-outs, at the top of Dean Street. They have been superseded by a hard-faced bunch of clownishly got-up damsels – black, white or coloured according to your choice – kids, merely, some of them, running after custom – infinitely coarse and frightful. Gone is the familiar 'Hello, dearie' and the Gioconda smile of the old-time tarts, and also the old price list: 'Twenty quid for half an hour' is the price asked for a trip with an African quean; hence the expression 'dear old London'!

No doubt, Soho to those who come in coaches on a Company binge is the world, the flesh and the devil. But not to me. I once spent several weeks going the rounds of the strip joints, porn exchanges and peep clubs: I wonder now how I survived the boredom. For sheer *tedium vitae*, there is nothing to beat it. Nor was I alone – I kept encountering a man who did nothing but read the London evening papers during these sessions – a dedicated newspaper reader who would surely be as manna from Heaven to a circulation manager.

In the eighteenth century, Soho was salubrious, a select place in which to live. Evidences of this remain, fortunately, in well-proportioned though cruelly over-used terraced houses, now needing protection, and others with the staircases and pine panelling intact, such as No 68 Dean Street. The house of St Barnabas, formerly the House of Charity, at the corner of Soho Square is a wonderfully preserved and maintained example of an eighteenth-century magnate's town residence. What was once the embassy of the State of Venice remains on the opposite or northern side, the whole district being gilt edged, first rate.

In the Victorian age came commerce, but very refined at first: Crosse and Blackwell, for example (if you find one of their dignified old brown stoneware jars with their incised names and address, buy it and keep it as a bit of old Soho) and James Newman, who made colours for John Ruskin. Soho was full of tailors in the 1920s, especially in Berwick Street, where Jessie Matthews began her career by dancing on her dad's market stall, and Wardour Street, before the film men arrived. Many of these tailors were specialists in one article; one would make only waistcoats, another dinner jackets and so on. Then, one could dine in 'faded corners of Soho', as in Compton Mackenzie's poem, for next to nothing.

Yet it was the day of great restaurateurs, like Leoni of the 'Quo Vadis', who would himself be buying in the markets at 3 am or, for special guests, going over to France for produce.

The ruins of St Anne's church, where William Hazlitt was buried, remind one of a later phase of Soho's life – the blitz – de Gaulle at 'The Café Bleu' and the Free French celebrating Bastille Day (Soho then being the only place where you could get a Gauloise), following all the foreign guests, distinguished like Mozart and Canaletto or unknown and undistinguished, who have found shelter in Soho.

With all this in mind, it is a matter for concern and anger that the quarter is fast deteriorating, the village-like life, the craftsmen and the old-established businesses disappearing. The trouble is that the people who live and work there did not start to fight the degeneration soon enough. 'Soho' was the battle cry of the Duke of Monmouth at Sedgemoor. And we know about him: he was fighting a lost cause.

33
Bow

THE FIRST sight of Bow Church gives one the impression of being at the end of some rural ride, where rustics still make fabulous remarks on the goings-on up at t'Hall; a view certainly familiar to Mrs Nickleby. At that time, Bow was still a village, but with imminent changes to be brought about by industrialisation. Yet, memorabilia of the vanished village remain here and there; there is a suggestion of it, if only in outline, in the buildings on the north side of the islanded church, and the King's Arms with its Georgian upper windows is quite clearly a country pub. After a long period of general debility, Bow is now smartening up. Some of its terraces of Bloomsbury-type character have been cleaned, and the rank grass and docks of the gardens replaced by roses and herbaceous plants: even the motorbikes, shrouded like phantoms in the front gardens, seem to be fewer. Nothing could be better for the area than the charming garden recently created in Bow Churchyard – an 'oasis' if one had the nerve to write it – a delightful garden of rest for birds of passage, feathered or unfeathered: without, an incessant thundering of traffic east and west; within, the flickering shadows cast by the plane trees on the old picturesque church, lush grass, roses of a quite unbelievable quality and the songs of birds. At the apex of the island, outside the churchyard gates, is Gladstone in bronze, gesturing with an open hand to the gents' lavatories below stairs at his feet – a ludicrous effect which could easily have been avoided. London books often have it that Wellington, mounted on Copenhagen at the Exchange, is the only London statue erected in the lifetime of the man. Yet W. E. G. was unveiled in 1882, when the politician was still very much alive, or so people assumed.

Bow has other Victorian relics to which I respond with enthusiasm, for example, the gable walls of faded superimposed adverts of entangled dim characters to be deciphered with difficulty, as on a palimpsest. Of these prophetic writings, perhaps the most legible is on a wall in Tomlin's Grove, 'Sunlight Soap Largest Sale on Earth'. But of the refurbished and improved Bow, by far the most striking example is the restoration of the Drapers'

Notice in the gents', Leyden Street, Stepney

Almshouses in Rainhill Way, formerly Priscilla Road – the whole scheme being a notable example of what can be done with historic but decayed property. Those responsible for the transformation were the GLC, the Borough of Tower Hamlets and various other bodies, all masterminded, so to say, by the Oxford Housing Association, an offshoot of one of the Oxford University settlements beloved of Victorian progressives. Seldom does one see such care for an old fabric shown by architects or craftsmanship by builders. The surviving almshouses, dating from 1707, were built under a bequest of Sir John Jolles, once Lord Mayor of London. Additions were made at subsequent periods, but the increasing industrialisation of the area led to the tenants being removed in 1867, by which time the group formed an enclave of dwellings surrounding a square courtyard. Over the years, parts were demolished or were left to decay. Now all that is left – the former chapel and flanking wings – have been restored to their original purpose as housing, but converted to one-bedroom houses and bedsit flats, the façades being scrupulously, even lovingly, retained and restored.

34
Tombs with a View

A LONG-TERM programme of restoration to the Highgate Catacombs, the entrance to which I illustrate, is in operation, and the entrance chapels are emerging from a long period of decay. Altogether, as a result of devoted efforts, the cemetery is coming back to life. The total value of present and contemplated repair and building work amounts to some hundreds of thousands of pounds from various grants: from English Heritage, from the Building Trust and funds from Camden Council for running costs. Much of the work is being done by young people, otherwise unemployed, under the auspices of the Employment Training Agency, a Government-financed body, which is achieving a significant improvement in the renovation of the cemetery.

The necropolis was laid out by the London Cemetery Company in the late 1830s as part of a general movement for the more sanitary and seemly disposal of London's dead, away from the over-crowded churchyards. It was planned and largely architected by Stephen Geary (who was later interred there); he designed cemeteries elsewhere and also the Holborn Wine and Spirit Vaults. The most dramatic feature of the Highgate cemetery is possibly the catacombs and their Egyptian-style approaches, but before Highgate got into the beneficent custody of the FOHC (Friends of Highgate Cemetery) these tombs were ultra-melancholy – enough to make one suicidal. I once took a party of young television camera people there to film it, and it subdued them for half a day afterwards. The short-lived Egyptian taste came in with Belzoni's archaeological discoveries in Egypt, and produced such fantasies as the vanished Egyptian Hall in Piccadilly and the delightful shop and house still preserved in Hertford. A similar wave at the time of the Tutankhamun tomb fathered several Egyptian *cinémas de luxe* and the Black Cat factory at Mornington Crescent.

Highgate, infinitely more rural, has been compared to Père-Lachaise, but the silences of the former are enlivened by the song of birds from leafy niches of thorn and bramble (it is a place providing for life as well as death), whereas the chief sounds of the Parisian necropolis are of the distant children in the Buttes Montmartre. What are these which are arrayed in white robes, and whence came

97

Egyptian entrance to the Catacombs, Highgate Cemetery

they? Why, Alfred Stevens, notable Victorian artist and sculptor, the great Faraday, gentle, melancholy Christina Rossetti, George Wombwell, circus proprietor and owner of the famous Nubian lion, Nero, whose portrait in Berlin woolwork hangs in my room, the highly polished coloured gentleman 'Hutch', Lillywhite, top-hatted and side-whiskered cricketer, and over 160,000 others, awaiting the general Resurrection.

Highgate early became a venue for sightseers. Today, it is highly organised to this end. No doubt, if funds are to be raised for restoration and upkeep, this is inevitable. Yet there is surely a novel way of fund raising hitherto overlooked. And that is to sell Karl Marx, gravestone and all, with a certificate of authenticity, to the Russians.

35

Tolmer's Square Revisited

WHEN THE Chief Planning Officer of Camden suggested I might like to see the new Tolmer's Square, I needed little persuasion: the old Tolmer's Square and the whole of that area immediately north of Euston used to be my happy haunting ground. I did not attend to my studies at University College with that avidity its authorities expect; I found that the apples from the tree of knowledge gave me heartburn. It seemed more rewarding to have a four-bob luncheon at the Express Dairy in Gower Street (where Flinders Petrie used to entertain his prospective Egyptian diggers to milk and a bun), have a fuddle in Simmonds', then at the junction of Gower Street and Euston Road – the finest second-hand shop in creation, and then head for Tolmer's.

It was next to impossible to loiter there and not believe the whole thing was occurring in a dream. An oval of finely proportional decayed houses enclosed a cinema, once a church, which showed films of the kind I prefer: '*I Married a Zombie* and '*I Was a Teenage Werewolf*'. To it hobbled old-age pensioners, not yet elevated into Senior Citizens, bent double, many of them, slopping in slippers, peering from below cloth caps, lugging bags as big as coal sacks. It was a place of dogs endlessly relieving themselves, dead-end kids, washing festooned over crocodile-cracked façades, crumbling porticos, eyes glittering from behind lace curtains and old women of twenty-five. Latterly came the squatters, by which time Tolmer's resembled the Spanish quarter of Naples with its vicious-ness subtracted. There's a lot to be said for living in ruins, an indulgence that reaches its apex of picturesqueness in the inhabited ruins of the Claudian aquaduct on the outskirts of Rome, for this is actually to bring to life the landscapes with ruins by Pannini, Wilson and the rest, in which figures point ambiguously to prospects or discuss stratagems in cloaks. Under my manage-ment, Tolmer's Square with its grass-grown cobbles and leaning Gothic lamp-posts would have been left untouched, to crumble slowly in the heat of St Pancras summers: London tourists, shunted from their well-worn tracks, would delight to immerse themselves in that rare blend of Pannini, Sickert and Phil May.

The new Tolmer's is as modish and smart as the old was shabby and atmospheric. The units, variously proportioned, are arranged round a central garden – the kind that attracts planners as fatally as it attracts cola tins and king-size fag packets – equipped with lamps like miniature Belisha beacons. Still, a good deal of thought, effort and money has obviously gone into it. The new brick-built Tolmer's is set against one of the great glass office blocks of the area, and this vast sheet of glass gives a curious effect from the opposite side of the square – reflecting momentarily the passing of the clouds in a moving panorama. These huge, glittering and dehumanising blocks have entirely altered the character of the Euston Road/Hampstead Road junction: only a fragment of the old terraces, certainly doomed, remains on the Hampstead Road, and I was delighted to see that this includes the former premises of J. Bryce Smith. Their name remains on the wall, though they were colloquially called 'The Artists' Graveyard' from their useful practice of selling the tackle of deceased artists.

Resurrected Tolmer's has been furnished with wooden porches of an idiosyncratic Oriental character at the areas, leading one to suppose them to be left-overs from some production of *The Tea House of the August Moon*. A final Tolmer's thought: architects, English architects at least, are not notable for the drawing of the figures they put into their perspective renderings; will they be likely to reinstate those old superannuated figures and cats and dogs and kids into the new stylish Tolmer's? Not, I fancy, on your Nelly!

36
Bermondsey Abbey

N THE gay old days,'sang Marie Lloyd, 'there used to be some doin' –
no wonder that the poor old Abbey went to ruin.'

So it was with Bermondsey Abbey, originally a Cluniac monastery
mentioned in Domesday Book, and given Abbey status in the four-
teenth century, by which time it had become very splendid and wealthy, just
ripe for Henry's hatchet-men. The Abbot at the Dissolution, however, made no
bones about packing up, and was handsomely pensioned off for his compliance,
bending, so to say, before the winds of change. Two English queens had died
there – Catherine of Valois, widow of Henry V, and Elizabeth Woodville, widow
of Edward IV.

Out of the materials of the demolished Priory Church was built Bermondsey
House, a mansion no longer in existence: it occupied the site of the market – the
so-called 'New Caledonian' – in Bermondsey Square, the whole area and much
else forming part of the Abbey demesne. Today, all that remains above ground is
the gatehouse at the west end of Grange Walk (note the iron hinges of the Abbey
gate on the stuccoed wall to the left of my drawing) and a fourteenth-century
silver salver preserved in the parish church of St Mary Magdalen.

A modern pilgrimage, with the antique market thrown in as well, if you go on
a Friday, is a London treat. The best way is to go down St Thomas's Street from
the Borough High Street, past Guy's and along the yellow-brick arcaded rear
wall of London Bridge Station to the junction with Bermondsey Street, which
leads directly to St Mary's, and across the market to Grange Walk. Bermondsey
Street was the ancient highway for pilgrims to the Abbey, but its great attraction
for me – I am afraid to write this – is that it is an entirely unspoilt Victorian
Street, one of the few unchanged, un-tarted-up streets in London – a place of
nineteenth-century warehouses and small terraces, all restorative to eyes
accustomed to the work of re-developers. Half-way down on the right is an
attractive group of stuccoed Georgian houses, next to a seventeenth-century
house with a charming first-floor projecting bay window and a curious weather-
boarded attic storey of the kind found in the houses of the silk weavers. Just

The Gatehouse, Bermondsey Abbey

beyond and a few yards down Morocco Street is a white-brick, purpose-built Victorian veterinary surgeon's premises, still with its original doors and displaying horses' heads on the façade, and the vet had a chair with his initials carved on. When I lived in Bermondsey and traversed the street almost daily – always with a connoisseur's joy – the cart horses were still going there for treatment. The charming early Gothic Revival façade and tower of St Mary's – surely the most delightful bit of Strawberry Hill Gothic in central London – closes the perspective. The rest of the church, seventeenth-century and older, is an absolute treasure.

When repair work was going on at the Abbey gatehouse, the builder kindly invited me in. Over the years, continual alterations have changed the character of the interior, but fine old beams remain. The tiny garden has been excavated for new drains. 'We have found all sorts of oddments,' said my builder friend, 'old bottles, clay pipes – broken, of course – and a huge tooth which may be some pre-historic animal's. Have a look for yourself.'

At this, visions of shards of Rhenish stoneware rose in my mind; perhaps a fragment, wonderfully carved, or a bit of Gothic tracery to beat the piece of cyma recta moulding I once found on the Appian Way. But my luck was out: all I discovered was a chunk of a Victorian jerry.

37
London Shops

A**S LONDON** becomes increasingly trendy, catchpenny and daft, I notice an alarming mortality among the steady old shops. One never knows which favourite shop of period character will go next. Today it is a high-class grocer's, still waiting upon families daily: tomorrow it has become yet another boutique, lurid in heliotrope and orange, catering for male, female or epicene – or all together.

Four establishments in which I took especial pleasure went in a matter of weeks. The undertaker's where they still provided horse funerals, if you were prepared to be embalmed while they got the horses together, was the first. Next came a certain marine store which I had long intended to record. It was run by a Persian cat, who eyed passers-by from a card table outside, while his ancient shop man dozed among a pile of junk inside. The paintwork, applied about the time of the Reform Bill, had faded to the colour of stale chocolate; no one ever seemed to buy there – there was nothing one could buy – and I often wondered if the whole concern were not a mere front for some un-English activity. Lastly, there were the closing of the lace curtain shop in Islington High Street and the disappearance of the two women who sewed in the window of 'The Original Invisible Mending Co. under Royal Patronage' in Vernon Place, Southampton Row. Those sewing females were as great a delight to me as the women who used to roll cigars in the window of Yates's Wine Lodge in Blackpool. As to the Royal patronage, I assumed it consisted of Queen Alexandra arriving with a landau full of King Edward's trousers to get the buttons sewn on at the close of the London Season.

I think that these nice old shops ought to have their virtues, atmospheric and architectural, more widely known. Quite a number are artists' colourmen. There is Cornelissen's, who removed in 1987 from their old Brunswick-green-painted premises (now a wine shop) in Great Queen Street to another Victorian shop in Great Russell Street; the interior is casually arranged yet workmanlike – nothing slicked up – and with ancient jars of powder colour in a showcase. Needless to say, you can buy things at Cornelissen's you cannot expect to find elsewhere.

Much the same goes for Brodie and Middleton in Drury Lane. One Bank Holiday, I watched their cat having a rare time scattering the powder colours in the window.

Particularly fine is Rippon's, the tobacconist and newsagent, at No 88 Dean Street, Soho – Adamesque doors with fanlights and delicate cable mouldings, windows divided into small panes and a superb Rococo fascia with characteristic Rocaille curves and leafage – entirely rare, superb and classed for quality with the former silk merchant's shop in Artillery Lane, Spitalfields.

New milk, pot plants and British budgie, St George's Circus

If a splendid early Victorian shop, complete and unspoiled, is your aim, visit Shapland's, the diamond merchants and silversmiths, at the corner of Newton Street, High Holborn. With its windows full of epergnes, salvers, vinaigrettes and the like, it belongs spiritually to the London of great town houses and carriage drives in the Park. Even the hanging lamps depending from the acanthus-crowned fascia are intact. It is unique and irreplaceable, the more so from its conveying no suggestion of being artificially preserved.

Among a number of picturesque ironmongers is Collins' shop in Earlham Street, with an enamelled announcement 'Sole Inventor of Elastic Glue' on the façade. It is, I think, the kind of hardware shop Gilbert must have had in mind when writing the fable of the aesthetic magnet who conceived a hopeless love for a silver churn. Earlham Street is, of course, part of Seven Dials, a long-neglected and increasingly shabby area that within these last few years has thrown off its apathy and become fashionable and up-market. I hope to God the trendiness fails to get hold of Collins' ironmongers, for this is one of the few genuine tradesmen's shops left in town. There are also the premises of Russell and Chapple, suppliers of various kinds of cotton and jute twills, scenic painters' canvas and the like, and a period undertaker's, both concerns being, as I take it, trend-proof.

The old silk merchant's shop, designed by a carpenter, Abraham Swan, in Artillery Lane was in this century a family grocers – Locke's. Local people called it 'the shop up the steps'. The cellar had an earth floor, and when Mr Locke gave up the business in the 1930s, the 'floor' of the cellar was found to be the resting place of coins that down the years had dropped through the cracks in the shop floorboards above. When the restoration of the whole was begun in the late 1960s, it was found that no footings had been provided, so that the whole shop and the living accommodation above rested only on the earth. A concrete raft was constructed to form a new and solid foundation.

38

Southwark

ONE BUT the most optimistic conservationists would, I imagine, travel hopefully across London Bridge in search of schemes of rescue and restoration. The up to the minute office blocks, gleaming in glass and granite, at the bridge foot and at the top of Tooley Street, seem no more than an extension of the deplorable Manhattan-like character of the City spawning on the Surrey side. Most of the London books, should they condescend to mention Southwark at all, do so only because of its history. They refer to Shakespeare at 'The Globe Playhouse'; Cardinal Beaufort, who took part in the trial of Joan of Arc and who lived in magnificence at the Winchester Palace on Bankside; Shakespeare's brother, Edmund, buried in the Cathedral; Chaucer at the Tabard, an inn destroyed in the Southwark fire of 1676, and so on: but they leave the reader with a general impression of a no-man's land, uninteresting for the most part architecturally and generally washed up with zero atmosphere, apart from the church of the Holy Trinity, a masterpiece of the Greek Revival.

A few years since, when the seventeenth-century, square bay-windowed house in the Borough High Street, the offices of a bottled coffee company, was demolished, I thought that the end had come, and that there was nothing left but for the whole of that area to become a developers' playground. Yet the opposite has happened: rescue and rehabilitation schemes are being carried out where demolition seemed inevitable; the reprieve and repair of Georgian domestic property, of Victorian warehouses built for the hop trade (Southwark's chief industry once, as Bermondsey next door was for leather and tanning), the careful rebuilding and restructuring of wharves along the river, and so on, in a sensitive manner is as praiseworthy as it is satisfactory. Even the Gothic 'Globe' pub by the market has come out in cleaned brickwork and new lamps for old. The warehouses opposite the Great Hall of Winchester Palace (the remains of which were restored in 1986-7 and thrown open to view) were in an advanced state of melancholy decay, presenting a sight of fern-festooned brickwork and corroding iron gangways across the alley – the whole gaunt and moribund. A new block,

Pickford's Wharf, with a stock brick façade divided by pilasters rising to a heavy classic cornice, an admirable essay in the style of the early nineteenth-century 'engineers' architecture', has replaced it to admirable effect: nothing could be better done. A similar transformation has taken place round the corner. Here the old St Mary Overies Dock, an ancient indentation of evil-smelling backwater and floating rubbish, overlooked by worn-out Gothic warehouses, has been superseded by an elegant block of Georgian character, the dock itself being rebuilt with a granite quay and well-designed iron railings to form an anchorage for the old three-master, the *Kathleen and May*.

All this can be described as conservation of surroundings, rather than of actual building. Of the last named, perhaps the most satisfactory is the renovation by Pear Properties in conjunction with English Heritage of the Hop Exchange. The building, occupying a long curving frontage to Southwark Street, is at once notable for the superb iron gates in the three-arched, pedimented entrance in the centre of the façade. The Hop and Malt Exchange was opened in 1868 to provide hop growers and dealers with a market close to the railway serving the hop fields. The current programme includes the restoration of the Exchange Hall with its decorative iron galleries, the Subscription Room and the West Wing to provide office suites for today's uses.

Union Street nearby seemed at one time about to disintegrate. Now it has come alive again as the result of a number of sensitive rescue operations. There is, for example, the Price Waterhouse Training Centre at No 14 – an old hop warehouse of stock brick with arches of red-gauged brick below the cornice – the finest and simplest Victorian commercial architecture now superbly restored and retaining the two hoists on the façade. Next to Chapel Yard is a group of three, all refurbished. The one next to No 14 was undoubtedly a Georgian merchant's house with living quarters above and a counting-house with Ionic pilasters on the ground floor, and the whole has been given a new lease of life by considerate handling; only the old hoist has disappeared.

Perhaps the most interesting resurrection job has been done on No 61 Union Street, which dates from about 1805. Very little seems to be known about its history, though the proportions of the upstairs rooms (these are awaiting repair and restoration), the shutters, detailing of the cornices and the serpentine staircase with its hand-rail of Cuban mahogany and domed well suggest a tradesman in prosperous circumstances. The premises belong to R. K. Burt and Company, paper merchants. No 57, across the entrance to the yard (which has its original gates), is actually an extension, planned by Mr and Mrs Burt themselves, cleverly reproducing and continuing the Adam-style shop front of the original part, the matching cornice and capitals of the half-round pilasters being carried out in fibreglass.

Also of note are two Regency shops almost opposite: No 62, with its ten-paned window and central gas bracket on the fascia, and No 64, 'Devonshire House', with its original 'Egyptian' block lettering in a reserved panel of stucco. Both shops have been repainted in the Brunswick green of the period. 'We are a nation of shopkeepers,' wrote Arthur Mee, 'who have somehow got on top of the world.'

Cornice and capital, Park Street, Southwark

39

'The Feathers', Hampton

THE FEATHERS', for some centuries Hampton's most famous inn, is now a private residence. No choicer spot could be found on the Thames. The long open reach of the water here was a favourite of the Victorians for yachting and pleasure-boating parties, as it is today of flotillas of swans, geese, ducks and seagulls, who conduct their affairs under the willows of the grassy margin and among the mooring places a few yards below the house.

'The Feathers' and its two lateral cottages were originally one building, the exact date of which is uncertain. I would date it to the late sixteenth century; in 1937, the Historical Monuments Commission suggested a probable date of late in the sixteenth or early in the seventeenth century. It ceased to be an inn at the end of the eighteenth century.

Near to 'The Feathers', as my drawing shows, is the parish church, built on the site of the dilapidated medieval church, which seems to have been of red brick and of the type frequent on the Middlesex shore of the Thames.

Farther down Thames Street from 'The Feathers', in the direction of Hampton Court, is 'Garrick's Villa', originally 'Hampton House'. It is actually a substantial mansion with a central portico and detailing in the Adam style, a villa in the Italian or Palladian sense and not that of the Victorian ribbon developer, with the domed temple dedicated to Shakespeare in the garden by the river on the other side of the road.

Here Garrick lived with his beautiful and adoring Viennese wife, Eva, in a completely successful marriage, which lasted from 1749 until his death in 1779. It was on his visits to Garrick that Dr Johnson, the actor's lifelong friend, would occasionally escape from his host's social circle to enjoy an evening at 'The Feathers', where he is said to have picked up the idea, subsequently suggested to Garrick, of constructing a tunnel under the road to join the villa's grounds with the river-side lawn and temple.

We know that Johnson, though no toper, was exceedingly partial to taverns: in fact he described an inn as 'the happiest contrivance of man'. The local story is

111

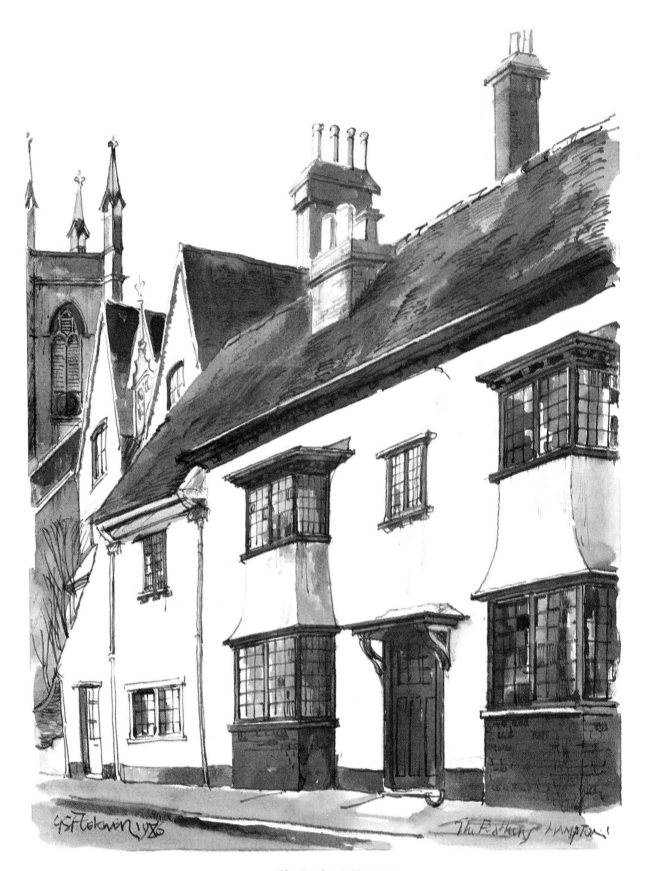

'The Feathers', Hampton

that his connection with 'The Feathers' came to an end as the result of a loan of ten guineas borrowed from a willing landlord by Johnson during a temporary cash embarrassment. Johnson omitted to repay the debt, in spite of a sharp note from his creditor.

When Johnson next stayed with Garrick, the landlord turned up to claim his due and 'in the midst of their altercation, Garrick entered the room, and learning the condition of affairs, paid the money promptly and showed the lender the door'.

'The Feathers' was for centuries parish property and a meeting place for bell-ringers on special occasions, whose libations were paid for by the church-wardens. From 1827 onwards, the rear part of 'The Feathers' was used as the village blacksmith's yard. In almost a century until 1920, when the smithy closed down, there were but six blacksmiths. In 1973, the parochial trustees decided to sell 'The Feathers', which had been parish property for more than three hundred years.

40

Backwaters

THE COLLECTING of London backwaters offers several advantages – low cost, variety, the charm of the expected – for one rightly anticipates such discoveries in London – and amusement combined with instruction, Victorian fashion. A collection so formed requires little maintenance, and if space is lacking, it can simply be stored in one's head.

Backwaters fall roughly into two classes: the one untouched by the human hand, the other tarted up into what estate agents used to call 'bijou'. Almost all are nineteenth-century artisans' cottages, and so bijou that one wonders how they all lived in those days of indefatigable confinements. Only London, as far as I know, has these *rus in urbe* enclaves in any quantity, except perhaps Athens, where similar nestling cottage dwellings on the slopes of the Acropolis are made delightful by creepers, figs and geraniums in old olive-oil containers – delightful but for the proliferating tourist-trap jazz restaurants. In Lancashire such little groups are charmingly called 'folds'; in London, they usually carry the name of the man who built them – 'Bloggs' Buildings', 'Grimshaw's Rents' and so on. The genuine unviolated article is usually found in the East End, north London and in parts of Pimlico. West End specimens are often too smart for a discriminating collector, or are becoming so, as, for example, Kinnerton Street, a complete village with long-settled inhabitants, corner shops and tiny pubs, unmodified until these last few years, but now showing signs of sophistication.

Some in my collection have disappeared, like the row of pretty cottages off Pratt Street, Camden Town, which I, like the man in H. G. Wells's sinister story, 'The Door in the Wall', have often hunted for, but never since found. Others, like Victoria Cottages in Deal Street in the East End, have become the prey of winos and squatters. However, I recommend the true type of the genre, a place of original flagged pavements, shaded with a willow and other trees, with tiny gardens mostly fenced by the authentic type of wooden palings, as they ought to be, ideally – the country come to town – Reed's Place in Kentish Town. You may start from the Tuscan-style London Railway Station at Camden Road, going diagonally to the corner of St Pancras Way. If you are lucky, you may encounter an increasingly familiar sight in London, thrown in for nothing – drop-outs begging under the railway bridge – unmindful of Henry VIII's having made them illegal. What is so striking about Reed's Place is its total contrast to near-by Kentish Town Road; the rural atmosphere opposed to the upholstered, pram-pushing women, the scent of cottage gardens instead of diesel fuel and hamburgers – contrasts that have a lot to do with the vitality that London generates.

Whilst in this stimulating region – for I reckon Kentish Town second to none for satisfying shows – you can find other rural backwaters. Behind the Assembly House in Leighton Road (a late Victorian pub alone worth the trouble for its fine engraved windows) is Falkland Place, a narrow, flagged passage with old (electrified) gas lamp standards, trees over garden walls and a little group of early-nineteenth-century artisans' cottages, and Leverton Street, with well-proportioned, Regency-type, terraced cottages, some with their original Greek anthemion balconies and gardens full of hollyhocks and ivies, the whole possessing a distinctly Chelsea flavour. I even found *Oxalis deppi* growing from a crack in the pavement, whereas in Kentish Town one normally finds only cola tins, empty crisp bags and the boxes that once contained the Kentucky chicken of the late Colonel Sanders.

41

Queen Square

THOUGH CERTAINLY Bloomsbury, Queen Square is, or so I fancy, the London square with the most pronounced Continental flavour about it. The others, with slighter foreign accents, are Sloane Square (and then only with energetic imagination) and Brooke's Market, the sort of dusty little square you may find around the Buttes Montmartre. The Italian Hospital, brilliant in white and red paint, has much to do with this. Its façade, displaying the arms of the House of Savoy, and the dome and cupola behind seem to have been transplanted like the apocryphal House of the Virgin at Loretto supernaturally from elsewhere. So odd it is to find it in Bloomsbury that the Londoners passing by seem merely tourists in their own city and the Italian working men and women who go there to be the natives. Yet the Italian Hospital was designed by an Englishman, T. W. Cutler, in the late 1880s. The Italian air is intensified by the running water from the conduit, which, although Victorian Elizabethan-style cast iron, reminds one irresistibly of those found in all Italian cities. This part of the square has been much improved by the Camden Borough Council, for not only has the conduit been put in order, but a paved area with trees and seats has also been created with the happiest results. The interior of the hospital has undergone extension and modernisation: a few years ago it had much more of a period character.

Through the trees rises the spirelet of St George the Martyr, a most interesting church of mixed styles; mixed because although built in the early eighteenth century – the original arrangement of a domed rectangle flanked by four columns remains inside – the church was brought up to date in the late 1860s and Gothicised, or rather Tuscanised, by S. S. Teulon, who also built the adjoining schools in that severe style he could use when required, as at St Andrew's Holborn. Though the exterior is a patchwork of styles, the church still has much character; the spirelet is a brilliant bit of novel geometry and very effective. The flower stall next to the Romanesque porch is another Continental touch.

On the other, the garden, side of Queen Square, a few eighteenth-century

Queen Square, Bloomsbury

houses remain, framing the lawns where lunch-time lovers carry on their *amours*, watched by pigeons, themselves not averse to a little gallantry, and on the summer afternoons, patients in dressing-gowns from the surrounding hospitals and nurses sit taking a breather or cross the square, cool in blue and white. The statue of Queen Charlotte (once thought to be of Queen Anne) surveys the sun-baked scene with mild benevolence from a bower of roses and climbing plants. She came to Queen Square in life to tend her husband, George III, during one of his attacks of madness. The square was then at the beginning of its healing career, and she kept a store of cordials, medicines and restoratives in the cellar of the charming eighteenth-century pub on the corner, 'The Queen's Larder'.

Also of interest is the association of William Morris with Queen Square. My own enthusiasm for him (except his Socialism – surely lethal to any other creative artist) is unbounded. But his many-sided, splendid gifts, added to his astute business sense, mysticism and dreary political ideas, make him – finally – a paradox. Morris moved to the old house in Queen Square in 1865, about the time that Teulon was up-dating St George's Church, in order to give closer attention to the affairs of Morris and Co. It must have been a wrench, accompanied by the severest withdrawal symptoms, for there was never to be a more perfect expression of the Pre-Raphaelite dream than 'The Red House' at Bexley which he left behind.

42
Smithfield

WHEN I told my butcher I was including Smithfield in these essays, he said, 'Not a patch on what it used to be... in 1932. Though the lorries were coming in, the meat was brought up "The Hole" from the railway depot by horses – three for a big load – a trace horse and two others – up the spiral incline. The butchers sold the meat off cheap on Fridays, in summer, and the hooks in the market shone like silver. And the pubs...the Manchester Hotel, where the butchers with money went, and "The Cock" in the old Poultry Market – down by the "village" – salt beef breakfast at 5 am. Everything was magnificent...not any more!'

Doubtless, but since Covent Garden ceased to be a genuine experience, and Spitalfields has got its marching orders, we have nowhere else to go, and there is still that blend of fine and humdrum architecture that subtle connoisseurs of London prefer. Smithfield – the smoothfield where the joustings mentioned by Froissart were held, the route the contestants took from the Tower being still commemorated by Knightrider and Giltspur Streets – had a bloody history before the meat trade. There was the stabbing of Wat Tyler by Walworth at the gate of St Bartholomew's, the death of Wallace and the burning of the Protestant martyrs, whose memorial is decorated by a tatty, faded wreath – not, I hope, symbolical.

I like to approach Smithfield from Cowcross Street, a name that suggests the bad old days of herded cattle in the streets, when occasionally a heifer would make a futile bid for liberty and be caught, with eyes full of terror, against some wall by its enemies – dogs and men. The disused original building, blackened and fly-posted, of the world's first underground station, dating from the 1860s, at the corner of the Farringdon Road was demolished in the spring of 1989. Higher up are two interesting pubs – 'The Castle', which has a pawnbroker's licence, and 'The Hope', notable for its etched glass. There were butchers' seasoning shops in Cowcross Street; one of them had a great spice mill for the grinding of mace and coriander. From the top of the street, one has a splendid view of the market in the finest Victorian manner – the rich cast iron of the

Grand Avenue, the splendid bracketed lamps and the clock, hanging from delicate ironwork that resembles the creepers of some tropical forest. Notice the colour scheme of the aisles – vistas of red, white and blue – red supplied by the meat, the white and blue by the painted ironwork. The market's pigeon population are distinctly rotund – by feeding on bits of fat.

Through the avenue, we can take in a panoramic view – the hospital with its eighteenth-century gate, spiritually belonging to Oxford, and the fifteenth-century tower of St Bartholomew the Less (the church itself being a feeble early Gothic Revival and possessing a curiously antiseptic atmosphere), the gateway of St Bartholomew the Great and on either side of it, Cloth Fair and Little Britain. No ancient buildings remain in Little Britain (there were still one or two, bomb damaged, until the late 1940s); yet, though its old fabric has changed since the days when Pip knew it in *Great Expectations*, the street still follows its twisting medieval path. Cloth Fair, originally for the sale of drapery, had turned into the great Bartholomew Fair by the reign of Elizabeth, and spilled out over Smithfield. Up to the Great War, Cloth Fair was a warren of narrow courts and ancient gabled houses. Of these, only two remain, rescued between the wars by my friend, the late Lord Mottistone, and his partner, Paul Paget, a truly civilised undertaking. In these Jacobean rooms, Lord Mottistone worked on his design for the restoration of the neighbouring war-damaged Charterhouse, assisted by his Cairn terrier, Teazle.

St Bartholomew the Great, only a fragment – largely the choir and crossing and part of the cloisters – of the priory founded by Rahere is as rich and solemn as a Bosboom drawing, infinitely interesting and wonderfully maintained. The priory gateway, where Richard II faced the rebels, was used as a stationer's in the early 1900s and was covered with signs and advertisements. A bomb in 1915 disclosed the timbering under the stucco, and the gateway was restored in the 1930s. I prefer it in its unredeemed commercial state, as seen in old photographs, rather than as now, a cross between the rear parts of Liberty's and the Tudor of Maida Vale. Yet it is picturesque enough. I saw it once in a freak snowstorm, and thought what a gift it was, under those conditions, for any Christmas-card artist who was quick enough on the draw.

43

On Tour in Deptford

WHAT I like about Deptford is that its population is entirely working class – or what was the working class before it took to the Costa Brava plane – in recognisably eighteenth-century surroundings; those in search of Georgian houses to tart up have unaccountably left it alone. Moreover, Deptford has a Royal and maritime past: Queen Elizabeth knighting Drake on board the Golden Hind, moored at the river end of what is now Armada Street; Peter the Great at Sayes, studying English shipbuilding, and his host there, John Evelyn; Evelyn's Royal master, Charles; Queen Victoria renaming the dockyard The Royal Victoria Yard; all of which gives the place an added interest, though nowadays the great ones of the earth have ceased to appear there.

Saturday morning or Wednesday morning are the times for the great Deptford walk, starting from the Harp of Erin, where the High Street begins. Towards the river is the old parish church of Deptford, St Nicholas (Georgian with medieval tower), where John Evelyn buried several of his children, with many touching thoughts of Christian hope and resignation entered in his diary – sentiments at variance with, but superior to, the morbid thoughts generated by the fearful sculptured skulls that top the gate piers. Deptford High Street packs more sheer vitality than any similar London thoroughfare. The architecture above the shops is of all styles – Georgian, Victorian, Edwardian, 1920s and 1930s. The shops below are a rich assortment of caffs, greengrocers, toy shops, take-away Chinese food, pets, bingo. There are the Salvation Army on the site of the Deptford Friends' Meeting House, where the Czar of all the Russias worshipped, Kennedy's pork and pie shop and, at the beginning of the street, Manze's eel and pie emporium – call there after studying the carved doorways of cupids and compasses in Albury Street. At Manze's, you can get into the Deptford mood, and have your jellied eels and pie and mashed, served with a generous helping of a curious emerald sauce, in a green-painted eating-box at a marble-topped table, marvelling the while at the bottles of non-brewed vinegar and the vast salt sifters which resemble lighthouses. Non-brewed, or alicker, the quintessence of the old working-class London, along with eels and cats' meat! There are good pubs here in which to wash down the eels, for instance, 'The White Swan', with a beautifully modelled swan in her alcove on the cornice.

St Paul's, Baroque by Wren's assistant, Thomas Archer, deserves a morning to itself. It has been marvellously cleaned, put in perfect order and is scrupulously maintained. A rose garden, also well groomed, leads up to the great semi-circular sweep of porch, a porch which seen against an indigo sky on a day of sun and rain is like the music of Handel – a triumphant assertion of the logic and order that lies at the heart of the Creation. Its big Roman Doric columns are as dramatic as those of Bernini before St Peter's, Rome; these and the two lateral Baroque flights of steps, to say nothing of the interior, would put St Paul's on the tourist's map, if only it were in Italy. But I never visit the church without thinking of a sparrow I once saw there flying from wall to wall, fruitlessly seeking an exit. Evidently, he had got in through a hole in a window, and could never find it again: the clergy told me that all efforts to rescue him had failed. Poor little fellow, frightened and eventually exhausted, intent on getting out of the house of God! Never, I thought, was the assertion of the porch more timely. . . .

Visit also the market in Douglas Way. Junk, hot dogs, livid Indian ornaments, bumper memo pads, jams and pickles of alarming hues, all trousers reduced. Bits of conversation, sawn off London lives: 'Six months now he's been in 'ospital and no one can find out wots the matter wiv 'im': 'Good shoes, these, Ma, uppers not up to much and they need solin' and 'eelin', but they're smashing value at two bob.'

From one end of the High Street to the other, you move immersed in the old genuine working-class London, wonderfully resistant to change, or so I hope: even the coloured population has becomes Cockneyfied. And if jellied eels or pie and mash are not to your taste, there is Kennedy's, the superb Edwardian pork butchers:

'Eat in the old fashioned way
With Kennedy's Pork Sausages
In Natural Skins.'

44

From Camden Lock to St Pancras

AMDEN LOCK, a curious mixture of Victorian warehouses, narrow boats and junk shops, is the starting-point for a recommended walk into London's industrial past. Dominating the lock is a magnificent warehouse which is exactly the kind of building that went for a Burton in the demolition frenzy of the 1960s and 1970s; today, happily spared, its future is, I think, fairly assured. It can be found just above the lock on the north side of an eighty-foot, cast-iron, roving bridge, which spans the canal at an oblique angle. (A roving bridge enabled the towing horses to cross to the opposite towpath.) The warehouse has a canal entry under a hump-backed bridge, allowing access by narrow boats and direct unloading without further transhipment after the Thames at Limehouse. Built by the Midland Railway in 1905 on the site of an earlier warehouse (probably built about 1868–74), it is a superb example of engineers' architecture in a mixture of pale vermilion and ochre-tinted bricks (blending at a distance into a soft red) with string course and quoins of blue brick. It as an austere grandeur and immaculate proportions that Palladio himself might have created; in fact, the warehouse has somewhat the character of a Florentine palazzo satisfactorily fused with that of a Lancashire cotton mill, with perhaps more mill than palazzo.

One can hope that the plans for the warehouse will mature, for about two years before the GLC disappeared, a rescue operation was considered for the 1851 granary at King's Cross. The GLC, the Museum of London and Camden were considering turning the granary into a canal and railway transport museum, with emphasis on the King's Cross area, re-opening the link with the canal, now filled in. But the scheme sank with the GLC, and the granary remains, if not friendless, then certainly aimless. Of course, these warehouses, like the canals and the docks, ought still to be used for their intended purpose, but the warehousing has fled to sites along the hideous motorways and out towards Tilbury.

The Midland Railway warehouse alone is worth a visit to Camden Lock, but there are other pleasures thrown in as a package deal. There is the lock keeper's castellated cottage, restored by the Waterways Authority, housing a charming

123

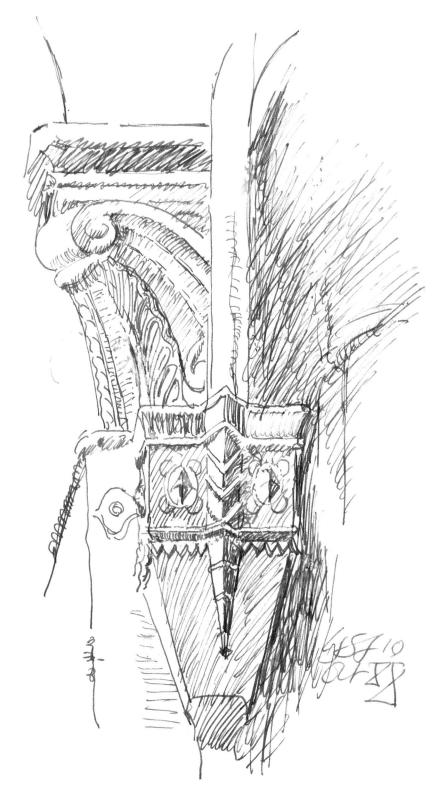

Rain water head, St Pancras

museum of prints relating to the Regent's Canal. After which, there is the towpath walk towards King's Cross among early and late industrial scenery, a curious but recommended experience, appealing chiefly to gourmets in search of unusual flavours. A variety of plants such as burdock and the sinister Japanese knotweed have established themselves on the walls bordering the towpath; up to midsummer, the song of birds is loud in the ivies and elders; the scenery unrolls itself in the manner of one of those Victorian panoramas. Narrowboats, turned into floating dwellings, appear uninhabited at their moorings, until a cat appears on a roof or a puff of smoke from a chimney indicates that the stove has been lit. The canal ducks are more put out by their own querulous tempers than by the thunder of the Inter-City trains going North.

There is a selection always on hand of London deadbeats. In April of 1988, I came across a Negro one-man band whose audience was composed only of mallards quacking in unison from the canal side, and shortly before that I met a punk family – a very punk couple and a baby with orange hair in a cockatoo tuft and huge ear-rings in its poor little ears. Eventually you come to St Pancras Lock with its totally Victorian middle distance – gasometers and the roofs of Scott's masterpiece, the St Pancras Railway Station – art and industry fused in a way that would have appealed to the Prince Consort.

45
Southwark Alleys

LATE AUTUMN afternoon when pale sunlight filters through the remains of the summer's roses in the Cathedral garden is, I believe, the right time to explore the Borough High Street; a time when old men doze or read tabloids on the seats between the buttresses, ready to reminisce, if you give them an opening – though not of the vanished galleried inns of Southwark, as you might imagine, but inexplicably of ration books and those shortages of cigarettes and razor blades and sentimental regrets for National Dried Milk and eggs. Alleys and cast-iron bollards were evidently a chief feature of the Borough, so that the Victorians could hardly go far without entering the one or colliding with the other. A surprising number remain for the enthusiast, though the continuing refurbishing and smartening up of old warehouses and former offices of hop merchants tend by contrast to give the alleys and yards an air of neglect.

The most dramatic alley is the Piranesi-like arched passage, with the Borough Market bollards dated 1813, leading to Green Dragon Court next to the Cathedral, but my selection of traveller's samples lies mostly on the other, the Guy's Hospital, side of the High Street. King's Head Yard, under a richly ornamented Victorian arch, is by the side of Beadles wine bar. There is a tanner's warehouse at the bottom end, but the chief interest is the late-nineteenth-century (1881) pub in the Tudor style, 'The Old King's Head', presided over by a lifelike bust of Henry VIII, realistically coloured, under a niche, all in the best Holbein manner. Next is White Hart Yard, which led to the great wooden galleried tavern mentioned in Shakespeare's Henry VI and described in vivid detail in *The Pickwick Papers*. Nothing remains today beyond the empty, forlorn premises of hop factors, but the yard has an interesting group formed by the backsides of old buildings, fronting the High Street – gables, ancient cement rendering, brick-work and a Victorian lamp bracket. Not to be missed at the entrance are the venerable stone bollards, very much battered and desiccated, which are certainly the last relics of the celebrated White Hart. Farther along is the yard of the George, the only pilgrims' and coaching inn of Southwark to escape total

The Grapes Alley, Southwark

destruction, the whole given a curiously Continental touch nowadays in the shape of big umbrellas over the tables placed for outdoor drinking customers. Opposite and behind the War Memorial is Calverts Buildings, a stone-flagged yard with a picturesque gabled house which was once 'The Goat Inn'. However, my favourite entry is that by the side of 'The Grapes'. All Georgian is the alley, with dark, furred brickwork, iron clamped, with bits of iron lamp brackets here and there, superb sand blasted glass on the lower windows of the pub and a wooden notice board announcing that they are 'Ancient Lights'. Here the London explorer can study a genuine unspoiled alley, complete with original granite setts and the wider pink granite border flags laid down for vehicles, the whole to a musical accompaniment of tinkling glasses and the cheerful rattle of plates.

46

Warren Street

NOTICE THAT a lot of my past experiences, thought to be gathering dust in the lumber room, have in fact been getting themselves secretly burnished – transcendentalised, so to say – and now appear as collectors' items. There are necessarily exceptions. The Festival of Britain, for instance, obdurately refuses to transmute itself even into rolled gold, but the British Restaurants are coming along nicely. My most interesting British Restaurant was just off Warren Street in a Victorian church hall, now demolished, or at least I fail to find it. The interior, lit by Gothic lancet windows, was colour washed in a lime green that first the years and latterly the cooking had faded and blotched into uncanny hues. Round the walls were texts in Lombardic capitals: 'Give an account of thy stewardship' and 'Let everything that hath breath praise the Lord' – the latter most fittingly, for on wet days the steam off the food and from the moist clothes of the customers rose like incense to the roof. Apart from a few students, the clientèle was also Gothic, ready made for medieval sculptors to carve into gargoyles, the whole thing (figures and architecture) being one of those subjects that seem to be created by a special providence solely for the convenience of artists – artists like Lowry and Sickert, for, of course, a Praxiteles or a Van Dyke could make nothing of them. The old men were so shaky and their National Health teeth so ill-fitting that the transferring from plate to mouth of the flinty potatoes and cast-iron beans was a voyage into the perilous unknown. When I once returned my fork to one of the servers, complaining that there were the deposits of two distinct dinners trapped in the prongs, she sucked it carefully, wiped it on her sackcloth apron and handed it back with 'That better, duckie?' I said, 'Heaps better. There's only the remains of one dinner now.'

Though all this has gone, Warren Street still has a lot to offer to the dedicated London lounger. Car salesmen – how they came to settle there is one of London's minor mysteries – and Asiatics appear and disappear with the unreal jerkiness of pushed-on figures in toy theatres, and at the Tottenham Court Road end are worn out, but once-elegant Georgian houses, desiccated, cut into, boarded up and weed grown in the areas, inviting, I am afraid, the kind of demolition and 'redevelopment' that has done so much to destroy the quality of the neighbouring Cleveland Street, where the Italian political refugees lived and the young Pre-Raphaelites sang revolutionary songs. Some of the houses are secured by iron ties, with wall plates on the façade; they have seen better days, and have that crestfallen air that suggests they know it. No 56, marked by an LCC plaque, was the home and studio of Charles Turner, the engraver who mezzotinted some of the finest plates in J. M. W. Turner's *Liber Studiorum*, which was issued in parts from 1807 to 1819. The artist kept an eagle eye on what his engravers were doing, and we may imagine his walking over from Queen Anne Street to this now knocked-about house to supervise the latest proofs and standing at the door, apparently an eccentric recluse, actually the innovator of a new and magical phase in art.

Almost opposite is a delightful shallow bow-windowed shop front, with the shop and house doors on either side in the characteristic London arrangement, and Adamesque fanlight over the door to the living quarters above the slender columns, the whole of the late eighteenth century and wonderfully, considering the area, intact.

Farther up Warren Street, the properties are in better shape than at the southern end. At the corner of Richardson's Mews, protected by a couple of unique bollards with pointed tops like sky rockets, is 'The Gurkhas Restaurant'. This used to be a shop where the present was the past – a gents' outfitters of unbelievably period character. Heaven knows what pre-Great War toggery they stocked, but I remember their celluloid collars and Jackie Coogan cloth caps of the sort seen in old street photographs. They also sold paper collars, a neck-wear once worn by impecunious clerks and rent collectors, but returning to favour in the early 1960s when the boys who played jazz in cellars took to them in a big way, buying up old flannel shirts and cadging collar studs from the aged parents.

On the corner of Conway Street is Evans's Dairy, one of the finest left in central London. Only a colour drawing could do it justice: the rich indigo/ultra-marine tiles, forming pilaster strips, with a cream inset; the gold-on-blue fascia, 'J. Evans Dairy Farmer'; the charming pastoral landscape panels in the tiled counter; the prosperous, clean as a new pin feeling of it all. This is another of the working-day mysteries of London – why the Welsh forsook their green valleys in the mid-nineteenth century, came up to town and took to dairy farming with cows kept on the premises?

47

Richmond

N SUNNY September days, I like to indulge in a favourite occupation – lounging in Richmond. I prefer to leave these idlings to this time, for then the withering foliage of water weeds along the river harmonises with the deposits of soft drink cans on the water's edge. The late roses and drooping sunflowers join with the Virginia creeper and pyracantha to make a rich orchestration of autumn. Clusters of grapes hang on the old brick wall at the Tudor gateway of the Palace: pigeons, gulls and crows pick among fallen leaves on the Green, where soft blue shadows envelop Maids of Honour Row and the surrounding trees. From gardens here and there, the robin twitters his plaintive *Nunc Dimittis* – his elegy for the fading year – goodbye summer, goodbye, goodbye!

Fortunate is London, having Richmond Green so close to town, for it is the very finest English scenery by special appointment, making us suddenly long for it, surprised by our homesickness, when it crosses our minds in some foreign place far away. The afternoon sunlight picks out sharply the details of cornices and doors of the eighteenth-century houses that unobtrusively but composedly assert their quality and distinction, as if aware that Time is on their side. The Green never changes. Neither, I hope, will Valchera's in the Quadrant, the only amendment I have ever noticed there being new wallpaper. The front of the restaurant – stained-glass panels and champagne bottles – 'Café Suisse' on the doors – cannot have altered much since the place opened in the misty days of King Edward VII. I used to go there with my Cairn terrier on Christmas Eves ('Velkom for ze leetle dawg') to feast, while old Rags snoozed under the table. Nowadays when I watch the sunbathers, kids and dogs on the Green, I am filled with a dreary sense of subtraction and hollowness, that no awakening out of his present sleep is possible, not even to go again to Valchera's....

Still, the lanes of Richmond are calculated to brighten one up: they are one of the chief charms of the place. There is Waterloo Place – its name gives its date away – a backwater of one-time artisans' cottages: how they accommodated the huge families the inhabitants then conceived, God only knows. Today this packing-in

Richmond:
English Autumn Afternoon

Richmond: an English autumn afternoon

is restricted to the tiny front gardens, in which are grown an astonishing variety of plants – roses, creepers, tobacco plants, marigolds – and some of the gardens have their original wooden fences or a copy. It is a backwater only in appearance, for Richmond people use it as City men use the City alleys, like rabbit warrens to get to somewhere else, mostly after shopping in Richmond Market, itself another and most picturesque alley, bursting with produce. A number of Richmond's lanes lead directly on to the Green, notably Brewers Lane and Water Lane. Water Lane, steep and paved with granite setts, lives up to its name, for the lower end is often flooded by the river rising in its winter and spring tides. There is an excellent pub, 'The Waterman's Arms', and a number of old warehouses, the lowest of which, now a restaurant, at the corner on the river 'promenade' appears in Turner's 'Richmond Bridge', once belonging to Ruskin and now in the British Museum. It is very agreeable to loiter here, along with the other idlers, sampling the holiday mood, watching the fishermen wading, the ducks paddling and swans attending to little niceties in the arrangement of feathers, all in the golden light.

Brewers Lane is given up to antique shops and American accents, and there is another good pub, 'The Britannia'; the brewers of the last century knew their business, and consequently there are few alleys in the old London areas without a pub. But the best of the lanes is, I think, Church Court, forming two branches that enclose the Georgian and Victorian parish church, where James Thompson is buried under a contemporary memorial referring to 'The Seasons' and 'The Castle of Indolence'. Shops come first in the Court, and these include the Café Mozart (where you will undoubtedly stop, if you share my regard for rich creamy cakes), then a group of eighteenth-century cottages and on the other side a collection of Georgian tombs, good enough to have been designed by Rex Whistler, dappled by the shifting light that filters from the close-grown old trees. Among them, appropriately, bearing in mind the several references to it in the Bible, is a stout branching old fig tree that stands by itself in its own little plot of land, a guardian, as it were, of the church porch. Today, too, there is music in Church Court: two young men, admirable musicians – guitar and saxophone, are playing old-time New Orleans blues that seem to become part of the autumn mood.

For years the area formed by George Street, Water Lane, the riverside and the bridge approaches was more lowering to the spirits than anything that ever came out of Basin Street. Years of neglect had brough this enclave of eighteenth- and nineteenth-century properties to a state bordering on desolation. Now the whole area has been restored and where necessary replaced by Georgian and Regency styles so lovingly (I write this deliberately), so skilfully reproduced that in a few years no one who did not know of its former broken-hearted condition would be aware of the rescue operation. It would have been so easy for an ignorant, vandalistic local authority (of which we have all too many) to have permitted a development of monstrous blocks of 'contemporary' flats and offices on the site, so destroying town and riverside promenade for good. Here, however, the precise opposite has happened: aim and method have been combined to effect a trans-formation amounting to a triumph of imaginative, sensitive, distinguished rehabilitation, unrivalled anywhere in my experience, even in Italy, the home of spectacular architectural resurrections. Even the tatty eighteenth-century house in George Street, used as a cinema, has been put back to square one, with a fine door Kent himself might have designed: like the rest, it has to be seen to be believed.

48
London Spas

I HAVE BEEN a spa enthusiast for a long time, and have enjoyed myself at a fair number of them – Bath, Tunbridge Wells, Cheltenham, Baiae and Plombiers – but a re-reading of Pepys has set me thinking about those around London, all moribund, I believe. Just now there is a great vogue for bottled mineral and spring waters, not only the old favourites such as Vichy, Contrexeville and the like, but also others from sources one has never heard of. Here, I think, are possibilities for some hydropathic entrepreneur to re-activate one of the London spas, bottle the waters and make a bag of gold – 'pure sparkling natural water, bottled at the springs in Collier's Wood', and so on. If Pepys revisited Epsom today, he would find the well right enough, but he would have to thread through convolutions of a housing estate, past electrically propelled milkmen, determined women with the wheeled baskets I call custard ambulances, pensioners and jeanagers, and he would undoubtedly order his coachman to Tunbridge Wells without delay.

The latest spa to be founded in London was Beulah Spa, Upper Norwood. I fancy it was perhaps the most attractive, though it had a very short life, from the 1830s to the 1870s. I saw it last a few years ago, when the only surviving building was the gatehouse, a pretty Gothic toy, and even that was threatened by demolition, but there had once been an assembly room and a pump house, all designed by Decimus Burton, who, like many Regency architects, worked as felicitously in Gothic as in Classic styles, with no cramping theories to inhibit him. The spa was in a glade charming enough to be presided over by naiads and other fresh-water nymphs – Horace and Virgil would have spotted them, leaning over the cool woodland spring – but they had fled long before my arrival. The tangled undergrowth of fern and blackberry made it impossible to find even the site of the spring.

Many of the London spas have disappeared without a trace, except for a name, and the sites builts over and obliterated. When I lived in Bermondsey, I used to walk up and down Spa Road marvelling at the totally un-spa-like character of the place, the spa having vanished as completely as the neighbouring abbey. The same applies to the once fashionable Bagnigge Wells in King's Cross Road, once the most famous of the several spas and pleasure grounds in the district. A stone tablet on the wall of a terraced house almost opposite the Police Station commemorates it. If you go there, in the direction of Riceyman Steps, you will need an active imagination to recreate those vanished arbours, rural pleasaunces and gravelled walks. The site was built over by Thomas Cubitt, the first of the great contractors, in the 1840s.

Hampstead's eminence as a spa is commemorated by 'The Wells Tavern' and 'The Flask Tavern', where the Kit Kat Club met and the water flasks were kept, which is why the present sign of a Napoleonic-period rifleman with a powder flask and an army-issue bottle seems a trifle incongruous. To my delight, the last, the very last, of the dedicated water drinkers arrived at the former well in Well Walk while I was there – burly, bearded and bent under a thousand-ton rucksack. The chalybeate water no longer flows, but ordinary water can be got from a humdrum chromium tap at the back of the fountain. From this, my pilgrim filled his bottle, sampling it first, rolling it round his mouth to savour the non-existent iron and then contentedly departing – faith, as St Paul says, being the substance of things hoped for. And if the tap water failed to do him any good, then neither did it do him any harm!

There were also many holy wells in London. Muswell Hill takes its name from the 'Mossy Well' where pilgrims came to drink the waters, commemorated by a plaque on the wall of a house on the site in Muswell Road. Clerkenwell is the 'Clerks' Well', still in running order. But the holy wells are another story.

49

Our Ragged School

S O YOU'RE admiring our Ragged School', observed a local businessman. 'Very nice – very Dickensian. Dickens had a great interest in the place; used to run jumble sales for them.'

To a degree, he was right, but not about the jumble sales. Vine Hill is certainly Dickensian. It was known as Mutton Hill when Oliver Twist was hauled up it to the Police Station in Hatton Garden, but the present building, in a style blending Victorian institutional with feudal Italian castellated, was opened in 1878, eight years after the novelist's death.

Few Londoners, I imagine, are aware of its existence or that the Field Lane Foundation still has its offices there, nowadays focusing its efforts at social amelioration, on caring for the frail, elderly and lonely in a number of homes and wherever distress calls for Christian welfare.

The Vine Hill School, now used as offices, remains almost unchanged; you can still read the faded lettering below the battlemented tower, 'Field Lane Ragged School and Night Refuge', though you will not find Field Lane, as this was swept away in the construction of the Holborn Viaduct.

Eminent Victorians, such as Ruskin, Lord Shaftesbury (who became the school's president) and Dickens, were great on schooling, and I wish I agreed with them. I think they merely saddled us with the curse of compulsory education and am not even sure that literacy is a necessary good: the inability of animals to read and write seems to me a benevolent protection against mass thinking, indoctrination and humbug.

Dickens wrote a vivid description of the school's earliest days in his piece, 'A Sleep to Startle Us', published in *Household Words* on 13 March 1852, at the period when destitute dead-end kids swarmed in rotting tenements, living by begging or stealing or on the chucked-out food scraps the early Victorians called 'broken victuals'. You see them in old photographs, white-faced, wretched, dreadful, the kind that were soon to attract the attention of the great Dr Barnardo.

'In this condition of things,' writes Dickens, 'a few unaccredited messengers of Christianity, whom no Bishop had ever heard of, and no Government-office

Porter had ever seen, resolved to go to the miserable wretches who had lost the way to them; and to set up places of instruction in their own degraded haunts.'

This was the first home of the Ragged School in West Street, Saffron Hill. Dickens's graphic descriptions of how the poor lived were efficient propaganda at the time; but they have had a curious side effect in as much as the Russians, devoted readers of Dickens, are convinced that such Cruikshank-like scenes are still to be met with in our capital.

Field Lane branched out into Industrial Schools in Dickens's lifetime, but the Education Act passed in the year of his death led to a division, the boys going to Hillfield Road, West Hampstead, closed in 1931, and the girls to Church Row, Hampstead, until 1901. Yet the Field Lane story goes on.

But when I reflect that today's kids would never be seen dead on a Sunday School outing – would rather play computerised games on the telly – I am inclined to a reversal: back to square one and that old unwholesome world of bread and dripping, gaslight and God in the slums. Elsewhere in this book, I have hinted that areas of Southwark, the Borough Market, for instance, will become tourist attractions, as will other parts of London that are either genuine, picturesque and neglected or down market and dilapidated. Prophecies are notoriously liable to misfire: H. G. Wells, though at times a true seer into the future, was frequently quite off the mark. I merely offer as a possibility, latent in the way London is becoming, that one day the Ragged School will become a museum of Victorian practical philanthropy...there will be prints, old photographs, blown-up engravings of a Dotheboys flavour, food tickets, records of rescue operations...scenes of the bad old days.

50

See It Now *or* Tommy Make Room for Your Uncle

ING'S CROSS as a name dates from 1830, from the building of a Doric copshop crowned by a statue of George IV, demolished in 1845. Previously the area (which included among its amenities the great London dust heaps referred to in *Our Mutual Friend*) was called Battle Bridge, a title still surviving in the road of that name. Here, according to ancient tradition, was fought the last battle between the Romans under Suetonius Paulinus and Boadicea, on the banks of the River Fleet. Whether the tradition is true or not, what is certain is that the knives are out once again in protest over the many hundreds of Londoners who will be affected by the King's Cross development scheme linked with the monstrous brazen plan to build a railway through Kent to serve a channel tunnel. The folly of a channel tunnel was the brainchild of a Victorian railway engineer, Sir Edward Watkin. Its revival today with the railway is, of course, a symptom of the mental disturbance of the English – our flight from reality. Considerable precedents exist for this kind of enforced dispossession: Louis Napoleon drove his boulevards through the homes of thousands of Parisians; Mussolini in Rome did likewise. They were despots. And whatever amendments are made, as a placebo, to the scheme, it is nothing more than naked totalitarianism, as cruel and as heartless as any that went before it. These things happen in England, because we, the submerged powerless, have almost unlimited powers of self-deception. In spite of experience, we continue to permit those whose calculations and ideologies leave no room for personal choice, let alone freedom from interference. Moreover, to our shame, we English do not combine effectively to assist our fellow men when a threat arises. We are glad that it is not in our particular backyard. The top boss men who get power over us as a result of our blindness are often helped by a type of petty Napoleon who cannot live without feeding a depraved appetite for power over others.

Those who are not directly affected by the present plans have a rich pleasure awaiting them by venturing into the hinterland of the north of King's Cross, an atmospheric, historic area of goods yards and offices and coal drops. There is the

Within the illustration: 150 PEOPLE LIVE HERE

GSFletcher
March 1989
Stanley Passage

Stanley Passage

magnificent granary of 1851–2 (venerated and written up by architectural historians – if only it were in Florence or Rome), Victorian flats (see my illustration and the writing on the gable wall), a whole complex of warehouses, caffs and industrial vistas and, of course, the gasometers of the Imperial Gas Company, themselves a landmark worth a pilgrimage. 'We are the gasometers,' I imagine them asserting, in a Kipling-like style, 'the great Victorian gasometers, the enemies of darkness and obscurity, for God said "Let there be light" and there was light – gaslight.'

Some of these features – the Granary, for example – may get preserved, if the pressures are sufficient. But if the remainder of this vast area becomes 'landscaped' (like the idiotic planting of trees on Lancashire slag heaps by those ignorant or ashamed of the qualities of the Victorian industrial scene), the remaining buildings will be stranded like whales in a setting purely artificial, unreal and stupid, to say nothing of the horrors of contemporary buildings, modish today, outmoded tomorrow, which will certainly surround them. In fact, the entire area ought to be left alone, apart from a measured amount of tidying up. That total loss of atmosphere and character is ours, the London adventurers. What it means to the ordinary people in the area and those in Kent whose lives and communities are to be trampled on is quite another matter. But in this affair between David and Goliath – Big Brother, that is – be certain that, in spite of protests, disinfectants, evasions, clap-trap, jerrymandering, Goliath will win. He has to, because David has nothing in his sling.

A snack at the 'Railway Café Restaurant' (walk north from below the St Pancras Station clock tower) is a recommended start to exploration. It has all the ingredients I favour: Gothic windows with lace curtains, plastic-topped, 1950-ish tables and a menu offering black puddings, eggs and bacon, Zeppelins in a cloud and so on – the real genuine London caff. After that, it is simply a matter of wandering, looking, appreciating. The Great Northern Granary demands careful study. Take in also a slice of the Caledonian Road – No 7, just beyond the Pentonville Road junction – the old forge, that is, built in the Aesthetic period, half cut brick, half tile hung, a novelty among the familiar stucco and stock brick. Balfe Street, still under restoration, has elegant small terraced houses of Georgian Bloomsbury or Dublin quality. On the opposite side of the Caledonian Road is the altogether charming Keystone Crescent, where a sweep's brush (now disappeared) used once to advertise the householder's profession. But see it now and the old London working class whose home this area is. You will not run into any of the bureaucrats, the planners and manipulators. They always live somewhere else.

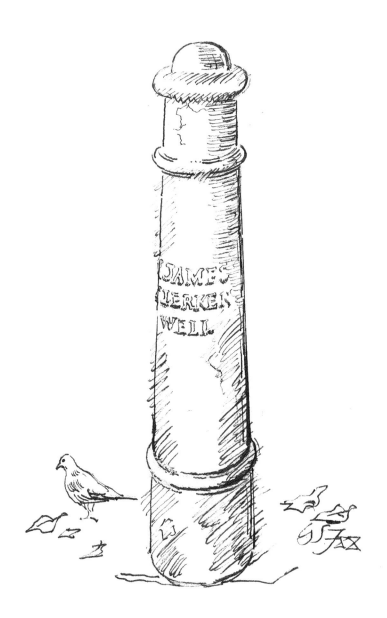

Bollard, Clerkenwell